THE HR
CATALYST

I0065270

THE HR CATALYST

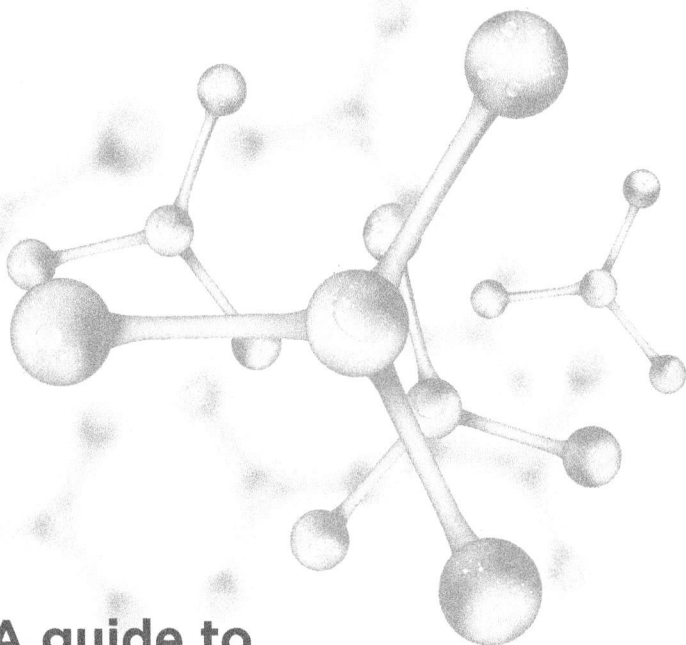

A guide to
the new practice
of leading HR

Callum McKirdy

Copyright © 2019 Callum McKirdy

Hambone Publishing
Melbourne, Australia

Typesetting and Design by Eggplant Communications
Cover Design by Daniela Flórez L

First published in 2019 by Callum McKirdy and Hambone Publishing

All rights reserved. No part of this book may be used or reproduced in any manner
without the written permission of the author.

For information, contact:
Callum McKirdy
callum@callummckirdy.com

www.callummckirdy.com

ISBN 978-0-6482011-1-3

Endorsements for *The HR Catalyst*

Callum McKirdy makes a powerful stand for HR professionals to reach their potential and for the industry as a whole to have a profound impact on business as we know it. This book outlines the new standard for best practice in HR leadership, as well as what to do and more importantly who to be to achieve it. Compulsory reading for anyone in Human Resources.

Peter Cook, CEO, Thought Leaders

HR Professionals have a timely opportunity to take the lead on cultural change that so many organisations are embarking on. The HR Catalyst provides practical tools and insights on how to achieve this with authority.

Gabrielle Dolan, Author of *Real Communication: How to be you and lead true* and *Stories for Work: The essential guide to business storytelling.*

I encourage all HR practitioners to read this book. I have worked with Callum over a number of years and come to understand his passion for the profession, but not as it is – how it can be. For many of us in HR, we have "a seat at the table", but how loud are our voices now that we are there? Are we credible when we put our position forward. Do we have the gumption to be the critic and conscience of the organisation? Callum has a new way of looking at HR. He challenges us to make an impact on the businesses in which we work, he also challenges us as a profession to be savvy, credible and for me the most important, to be influential. Can you walk out of the business today and say "These are the changes for good I made while I was there." This book pushes us to make that difference.

Linda Hart, General Manager Human Resources,
Healthscope NZ Ltd

HR functions have been in strife for a while and unfortunately, they can be their own worst enemy. Often with an internal focus, they don't look outwardly to see if the business is really getting what it needs. Frankly, they are in denial. Callum has provided a simple roadmap for HR functions to get back on course, demonstrate leadership and provide true business value. A must-read for any practitioner wanting to make a difference in the work they do and have pride in their profession.

Donna McGeorge, Speaker, Trainer, Author of
The 25 Minute Meeting

Contents

INTRODUCTION

It's time!

The not-so-unspoken truth about HR

This book was originally titled *Strategic HR 2.0: Influence with Impact,* but it's more than that. A whole lot more. The intention for an HR professional should be not just to influence change, but to be the catalyst that causes that very change. This book emerged from a deep desire to turn the Human Resources profession around – in particular, its reputation for talking a good game, but never really delivering.

For a long time in my career I was embarrassed to tell people I worked in HR. I would say I worked in "leadership development", or at a particular organisation, hoping the follow-up question wasn't "Oh, so what do you do there?" I was, for a decade, running from HR.

In setting up my own consultancy in 2013, I initially called upon my network of HR leaders for work in their organisations. Thankfully, many obliged, and while I put food on the table for my growing family, I was also thrust into the incredibly privileged position of seeing HR from a slightly more 'outside-in' perspective. Working with teams and leaders spread far-and-wide across organisations enabled me to spend several years asking one very pointed question once or twice per week: "What do you think of your HR function?"

From the answers I compiled I not only found myself drawn back into the profession, but also actively defending HR. Having spent some time out of the firing line, I now saw the untapped potential the people profession had to offer. You see, I commonly heard something like this:

"Our HR team has a 'Do as we say; not as we do' attitude".

I'll expand on this soon, but at the time I was starting to think there was something bigger at play than simply a brand issue. What I was hearing was that HR as a profession lets itself down and gets in its own way - not through a lack of technical skill or knowledge, or even a willingness to be better, but in the way we go about practicing HR. We would espouse best-practice, but rarely would we be seen to put such advice into practice ourselves. What's more, every HR team I ever worked with seemed to quietly admit this in some way, shape or form in the safety of the HR office. I found myself getting caught up in this curiosity. This private admittance of our shortcomings seemed to bring us together – HR as its own little community, keeping itself safe. And so it should, but not to the detriment of the impact HR can have in the business.

I started to explore this some more. Over the past two years, while reigniting the spark for HR and deepening my respect for savvy practitioners I've worked with, I began to notice some common traits of a somewhat exclusive tribe of HR professionals – a tribe that seems incredibly effective for how small it was. With some commitment and dedication, this group appeared to have the potential to grow into the new wave of people professionals that could redefine, reframe and rebrand HR.

Regardless of age, experience or tenure in a given role, and irrespective of whether they specialise in a particular area of HR or perform generalist roles, some practitioners just seem to be able to create lasting change with the people they work with across their organisation. I set about trying to capture and define the characteristics displayed by this group of highly effective practitioners. The result is my *Catalyst5 HR©* model of HR practice, which comprises the remainder of this book.

Interestingly, these five traits do not necessarily shine through more at senior or leadership levels within the HR fraternity. They are almost career and success-agnostic. They are infinitely learnable, which makes them accessible for you as an HR professional, no matter what stage of your career you're in. A word of warning, however. By virtue of being learnable, they are also equally unlearnable. This is not some magic bullet that you can read once and then be on your way. To make Catalyst characteristics stick, we must make them habits.

The case for change

Let's take a step back, as it's time we faced some truths about the HR profession. I reckon the first of these truths we must both acknowledge and own is that Human Resources is a leadership function. Regardless of your role or responsibility, you have the opportunity – and the responsibility – to lead those around you. This is not a widely accepted view, both within and outside of HR circles, but it should be. With the ability to touch every corner of the business – a privileged position shared by no other function – it really is up to HR to directly and indirectly lead the way in enabling people to be the best versions of themselves. Yet more often than not, we don't. This is not for want of trying, nor is it due to a lack of talent, ability or skill.

Regardless, HR is simply not fulfilling its wondrous potential as the driver of business productivity and success. If we're honest, we[1] know it. We can't ignore the truth:

---

1   You'll note the way I refer to "we" – I'm owning this too as I've been in and around Human Resources for almost 20 years. I'm part of this issue and I intend to be part of the solution, hence this book.

Right now, HR is not driving the people agenda.

Our profession's own positioning as first, the trusted people advisor, and then as the strategic business partner, was lost long ago to technology. Continued renewal of technology application is superseding people as the perceived leverage point for future success in the minds of CEOs and Boards of Directors. At best, people are still talked about at these levels. Yet for several diverse reasons, very few decisions and little action occurs with people front-of-mind, not least because HR has lost its seat at the top table.

Ten years ago, we were close; now HR has once more slipped down a tier or two. We accepted this snub because we bought-in to the rhetoric that "this positions HR closer to the people". Rubbish. We even outsourced development as we attempted once again to define what HR is about and be more strategic, when what we should have done was doubled-down on the people factor. As a result, our position to lead the one true lever of influence – organisational culture – is tenuous.

This worries me – not the stepping up and owning part of the problem, but the fact there's such a problem in the first place. I mean, what were and are we thinking? How did we let this happen? More to the point, how did we make this happen, and why?

We can blame the incompetence of managers and leaders across the organisation who we think "just don't get it". We can blame other functions like Finance, IT, Marketing when we all competed for air time with the CEO, but the truth is they won. They were the more savvy, better hustlers... they out-clevered us. Good on them. We were out-positioned by other functions because we couldn't work out what ours was. Therein lies a massive problem, but also a huge opportunity for our profession.

What did HR do? Well, we spent too long arguing for the people agenda to be everyone's responsibility; that HR was there to support but not 'do for' managers. Instead of confronting culture head-on and leading the way by owning our responsibility as the experts of how organisations adapt, sustain and thrive in the VUCA economy. We spread ourselves so thin that we ended up confusing even ourselves, muddying the waters to the point we no longer know what HR and its role is. We told businesses they could do what they want. Just because the cool kids like Google, Uber and Zappos were doing crazy things, doesn't mean those things will suit all workplaces. HR got carried away with the enthusiasm of the business in thinking that those same ideas will work for them. Instead, we should have explained why those organisations are different, and guided the team to an appropriate strategy. We went along with what our customers *wanted*, instead of standing firm on what they *needed*.

The predicted future skills for HR are (mostly) wrong

In business we now trust data over people, because our assumption is that technology provides both security, and assurance that the bugs have been worked out of the system in the development phase. Yet people come with bugs built-in! Indeed, this is what makes organisations and HR itself so incredibly dynamic and exciting. What this now means is the chief data gurus and technology wizards have free access to the CEO and are increasingly being appointed to Board level roles, while HR needs permission to speak *through* a collective corporate role that, more often than not, is a numbers, not people person.

In fighting for too long to be strategic we missed the perfect opportunity to influence. Yes, strategy is critical, but not all HR professionals need to be as strategic in the same way the HR Director or CHRO must. Unfortunately, we somehow failed to clarify the distinction for many practitioners and this saw them flail rather than fly. Many HR practitioners yearn to be more strategic, and are told they should be, without even knowing what that means.

We have, in recent years, taken a similar approach with HR technology – that all HR people must be tech-savvy – when the reality is we must ensure whatever technology we implement actually adds value to, bolsters and drives the people agenda (and that HR people understand the distinction). Our aim is not to produce outcomes or behaviour that distracts people from getting good work done. It's about the credible use of technology to drive the organisation forward. We lost sight of this in our 20-year quest for strategic credibility. I now fear we're doing the same with technology – and people have noticed.

The real oil

Executives are being told "data is the new oil", when in fact people are the new oil. They always have been, but you knew that right? Great people that are 'right' for your organisation are finite and scarce, at least in the context we're discussing here. Data is simply the current fuel source (like oil) that enables people to do stuff – better, more efficient *stuff*. People remain the key driver of organisational success and will for a long time to come.

Culture is about people thus the vibe, rituals, artefacts, symbols and behaviours of an organisation is the collective key lever in business productivity. Tasks are indeed being replaced as technology develops, but jobs themselves are also being re-engineered to generate greater results and outcomes. So, what we're facing isn't a technology issue; it's a people issue. In fact, let's stop calling it an issue – it's an imperative!

> People are the future of work, and HR must lead that future.

The place ideas go to die

Business is tired of waiting for HR to lead. A report from Berzin by Deloitte in 2018 confirmed that designing the organisation of the future is a top challenge for business executives around the world. Given that right now, HR isn't there, we can only assume they are going to do this themselves. Whether it's with a technology-driven focus, or at least without senior HR representation and input in the critical ideation and design phases – if not the entire transformation process – the business world is moving on.

This same report did go on to say that the best performing HR functions had a focus on *developing their own teams*, suggesting that if we focus on *how* we go about HR *together*, we might just have a shot at proving our worth. I think that's a shot worth taking.

An article in Fast Company back in 2005 titled *Why we hate HR* professed:

> "HR is the corporate function with the greatest potential — the key driver, in theory, of business performance — and the one that most consistently underdelivers."

It went on to say:

> After close to 20 years of hopeful rhetoric about becoming "strategic partners" with a "seat at the table" where the business decisions that matter are made, most human-resources professionals aren't nearly there. They have no seat, and the table is locked inside a conference room to which they have no key. HR people are, for most practical purposes, neither strategic nor leaders.

Ouch! 14 years on and that still hurts. But the truth has a habit of hurting, right? Early in 2018, at a conference in Melbourne attended by leaders and business owners, HR was referred to as "The place ideas go to die". While this is a sad indictment on the profession, what was sadder still was the fact nobody defended HR. Human Resources is a leadership role. We have to start thinking of it that way and leading it with a renewed passion so that our reputation can be turned around. That starts with those of us who 'do' HR owning our profession, our foibles and standing up for it when it matters. That starts now.

Reaching peak overwhelm with skill acquisition

The easiest thing to do in HR is to recommend the further development of a particular skill, in order to build credibility by doing a better job in a technical sense. Develop your analytical skills, or maybe proficiency in a particular coding language. Learn how to type faster, reverse a forklift, or pile on the knowledge of specific legislation. We read headlines like "Key Trends" that draw us in and demand tht we develop certain skills to keep pace with those trends. We are motivated to read and share articles that espouse the fad-skills that HR practitioners require to be relevant.

No wonder HR has a reputation for not doing anything. Our problem is not a lack of skills, therefore the solution was never going to be found in simply upskilling ourselves. We need to do something with the skills we have, turning our energy instead outwards towards helping the business around us. The potential for great work is so large we struggle to decide where to focus our limited time, energy, resources and attention. New, cool opportunities arise every day, which we could and often do jump on, without really weighing up the pay-back.

In 2017 CIPD advocated for HR to:

1. Demonstrate the value of the HR agenda.
2. Use HR data to strengthen evidence-based decision making.
3. Harness the benefits of technology.
4. Prepare for economic uncertainty (for example globalisation and Brexit).

5. Adapt to the changing needs and desires of the workforce.
6. Strengthen the capability of people managers.

Also in 2017, CIPD's Australian counterpart AHRI reported that CEOs expect HR to:

1. Anticipate and lead change
2. Live and breathe professionalism and credibility
3. Show value through behaviours more than knowledge
4. Be more self-critical
5. Champion the genuine care of employees

Most of the above lists comprise behaviours we need to adopt and/or bolster. It seems these speak more of a need to develop *how* HR is performed, than *what* it is HR actually does.

Enter the HR Catalyst: The New Practice of HR

HR by its very nature is a strategic function, but not all HR practitioners need to aspire to being strategic. We must all have an appreciation for and awareness of the bigger picture, as well as where and why HR does what it does. What we need to be careful of is that this strategic line-of-site doesn't supersede or hinder HR's primary focus of being *of service* to the business by being *in service* to individual customers each and every day. Sometimes we fight this notion fearing it will dilute or dumb-down HR's positioning. On the contrary, we should double-down on this. In other words, let's influence towards achieving business goals by doing some exceptional work with the people that matter. Essentially, we'll be having far greater impact as a result of how we go about our work in HR, rather than relying solely on technical nous and trying to constantly position ourselves as experts. That much is a given.

I call the practitioners who take this approach *HR Catalysts*. These are the people in HR who spark and lead sustainable change in others across the business. This is who we want to be.

The concept of a catalyst itself is commonly used in chemistry and is defined as *a substance that increases the rate of a chemical reaction without itself undergoing any permanent chemical change*.

This is interesting when applied to human characteristics. We think leaders need to demonstrate such characteristics and often describe leaders as creating environments for people to be the best version of themselves. I believe this also applies to the Human Resources profession – this is also our responsibility. We're here to enable workplaces where people can thrive through the provision of advice, tools and direction that sees managers and leaders creating optimised people-centred and outcome focused environments. Now that's waffly HR-speak if ever I wrote it!

Indeed, more simply, the Collins English Dictionary defines a Catalyst as:

> "*a person or thing that causes a change or event to happen*".

HR itself is known for starting a lot of things; it's also known for not necessarily seeing those things through or for clearly communicating the purpose behind these initiatives such that customers clearly see the need for them.

Often, a catalyst is described as a person or thing that precipitates an event. Precipitates is important here also, which means *to cause something to happen quicker than it normally would*. This is not what HR is known for, but imagine the impact you could have should you choose to take up the challenge of becoming an HR Catalyst? Imagine the surprise in turning around the status quo reputation of our profession, let alone the personal motivation in knowing you are operating above the expected average?

Catalysts go further than activists

Dave Ulrich refers to practitioners operating in this manner as "credible activists". Activism is all good, but it's only one side of the virtual coin. This suggests that HR's role is partly to take a stand for what's important, but stops short in conveying credibility by "getting stuff done"; especially stuff that matters in a given business. Raising awareness is one thing; getting stuff done is another. Catalysts do both.

It's the 80:20 rule professionalised. Created by Italian economist Vilfredo Pareto, this principle describes how across many fields, 80% of the effects come from 20% of the causes.

Catalysts intentionally focus their attention on a few key priorities (be they projects, people or places) and commit 110% to them, because they know they matter (they've done the research and banked the data). Yet, Catalysts also know when to let go of a project that is not gaining traction. They keep an eye on reality and can quickly pivot from one line of work to another. Catalysts filter input and feedback to decide what is useful and then build momentum with their cause by creatively and perceptively working through people doing so in genuine and empathic ways. In essence, the HR Catalyst is the consummate professional – savvy, credible and influential – a role model of the behaviours that drive businesses forward.

> Indeed, HR Catalysts step into HR's leadership role by being the impetus and the agitator of purposeful change within organisations.

HR Catalysts aren't new per se, but identifying their practice is something that has not been fully recognised. Now, more than ever before, HR requires a shift in behaviour. It's time to level-up our practice and go about the doing of HR that delivers on the potential our profession has been waiting to unlock. Yes, HR Catalysts have been working in organisations for some time now, we just haven't identified them and given them the credence they deserve. Now, more than ever, the work tendencies and behaviours of catalysts is required to change the game of HR; to demonstrate the full potential of the HR profession and build our reputation as the owners of the people agenda.

The future of organisational success is riding on a new way of doing HR. It's time Catalyst HR practice became the new normal in the profession – the way all HR professionals practice.

So how do we do make this change? HR Catalysts practice through five key competencies. While these competencies may apply to other professions too, these are the ways of practicing our profession that separate highly-effective HR professionals from those that are simply highly-skilled. The point of difference for an HR Catalyst is application – the doing, the implementation, the actions undertaken, the actioned learnings, the behaviours applied to working in the field of Human Resources. These then are turned into ways of being – personifying the characteristics of a Catalyst HR practitioner.

This is best summarised using a *Be – Do – Have* coaching model, as popularised by Louise Hay, Anthony Robbins and Stephen Covey. This fantastic model has been widely used across coaching circles the world over for decade, whereby who you are *being* informs what you are *do*, which in turn informs what you *have*.

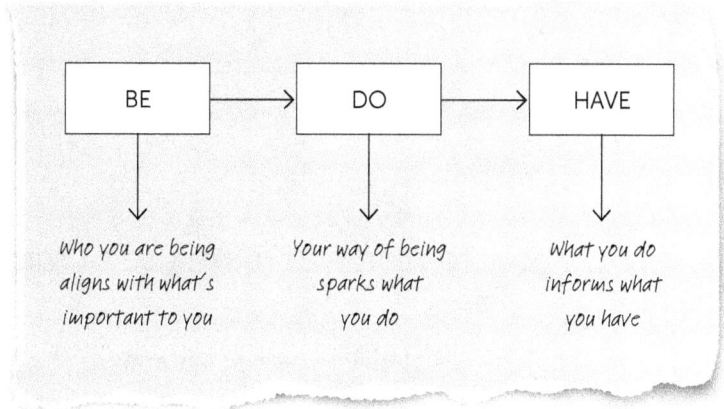

```
┌──────────┐      ┌──────────┐      ┌──────────┐
│    BE    │ ───▶ │    DO    │ ───▶ │   HAVE   │
└──────────┘      └──────────┘      └──────────┘
      │                 │                 │
      ▼                 ▼                 ▼
 who you are being  Your way of being   what you do
 aligns with what's   sparks what      informs what
 important to you       you do          you have
```

We'll talk more on the concept of your HR brand later, but for now just ponder the idea once more that for the HR Catalyst, who you are and how you behave informs what it is that you do. This is what people notice and remember you for. Your credibility is based on the way you are you around them.

In terms of *Be – Do – Have*, the HR Catalyst requires the following five ways of being, which we will cover in descending order throughout the remaining chapters of this book:

BE	DO	HAVE
Insightful	Understand	Greater Empathy
Unattached	Surrender	Deeper Wisdom
Focused	Hustle	Meaningful Progress
Connected	Collaborate	Stronger Connection
Yourself	Believe	True Presence

A note on how to read and make use of this book

This book is a guide about how to be an HR Catalyst, so the chapter headings will be labelled as they are in the 'BE' column above. Each chapter will describe ways of working – what you need to 'DO' in order to be known as an HR Catalyst. You will also note that the term *customer* is used through each chapter. This is in reference to HR and the wider people profession being both a leadership and support function – there to serve member of the organisation. As such, all managers and staff who make use of HR's services – whether directly or indirectly - are customers. This does not dilute HR's potency or effectiveness; rather it sharpens the professions focus on being people-centric with an outcomes-focus, and should do so for you, the emerging HR Catalyst, too.

The chapters that lie ahead are actually based on the five dimensions of the Catalyst5 HR© model, which began as a programme run publicly and professionally in-house across New Zealand and Australia. It emerged from almost 20 years in and around the HR profession. This was time in advisory and business partner roles in the public sector; as an HR Director in a large not-for-profit; consulting and leading change initiatives for a Big-Four consulting firm, before establishing my own leadership and culture development company working predominantly with HR leaders and their teams to affect change in their organisations. Over the years, I witnessed time and again HR never reaching or delivering on its potential. This is a potential everyone knows is real – CEOs, C-suite executives, HR professionals at all levels, and even the detractors of HR across organisations. There is no question HR has a legitimate reason for existing, the trouble is HR has lacked a process for getting out of the rut we have dug ourselves into by focusing on building technical skill (the WHAT) over the real need to own our behaviour (the HOW). This shift in focus is where the future of the profession really lies.

The behavioural dimensions of the Catalyst5 HR© model stack like building blocks – meaning they add to the previous dimension while taking something from it at the same time. Development of each dimension requires the same process of first seeking deeper *insight*, then being *unattached* to anything that is holding back your better practice. From there you will *focus* in order to achieve more with a project or person, enabling you to grow stronger *connections* with those you must work with and through, and ultimately be *yourself* so that this practice is easy, natural and sustainable for you.

You can use the five dimensions in this model, and the sequence in which they are presented, as an approach to educate non-HR people across your organisation in a way that positions you as influential and as having impact. In a nutshell, if you are able to help a manager you work with to understand what they need to let go in order to have greater traction by focusing on the relationships that person needs to prioritise, and how they could go about this with authenticity, not only will that manager thrive, but your brand and reputation as an HR Catalyst who sparks lasting and worthwhile change in others will flourish.

What this means for you, dear reader, is this book can be opened up at any chapter and you will find tips and questions available for you to immediately apply to your HR practice. In a sense, you can't not gain from applying the principles that follow! Afterall, you're a savvy professional with catalyst tendencies. You wouldn't be reading this book if you weren't.

So, let's get to it. It's time we unleashed the HR Catalysts among us.

CHAPTER ONE

Insightful

BE	DO	HAVE
Insightful	Understand	Greater Empathy
Unattached	Surrender	Deeper Wisdom
Focused	Hustle	Meaningful Progress
Connected	Collaborate	Stronger Connection
Yourself	Believe	True Presence

Insightful

> "The illiterate of the 21st century will not be those who cannot read or write, but those who cannot learn, unlearn, and relearn"
>
> – Alvin Toffler

To understand something means *to perceive the intended meaning of* (words, a language, or a speaker) or *the significance, explanation, or cause of an action*. It means to comprehend what's going on. Further, understanding means to develop a sympathetic awareness or tolerance. Many HR practitioners strive to understand concepts, people, and technology as they impact their organisation, but few turn that knowledge into *insights*. Often in HR careers, our ability to create the latter is quickly beaten out of us by the sheer overwhelming number of options, opportunities and opponents to what HR is trying to achieve. We get caught up in the busyness that consumes our ability to really think about what the organisation is trying to achieve. As a result, we operate at the surface level in most tasks, never going very deep. Unfortunately, we've treaded water for too long, until it's become what we are known for.

It's a real problem when HR as a function gets relegated to simply being able to provide transactional services. For example, HR professionals battle with the competing demands of difficult managers who expect strategic advice but treat you as a glorified administrator in a recruitment process. Often, we accept this as just a necessity of the role that everyone has to put up with. HR Catalysts, on the other hand, form insights from their interactions with customers;

bridging what they are trying to achieve with a service that enhances both the experience and achievement of goals. The HR Catalyst does not pander to every random idea and request to fetch someone's personal file. Without insight, the work of HR is all the more difficult, and fundamentally unable to be a value-add service.

The *Insightful* dimension of the *Catalyst5 HR©* model is an important first step in developing your ability to spark change in others, and comprises three key elements:

1. Big picture context
2. HR business acumen
3. Your own HR practice

Each is critical to a Catalyst's practice because they arm the HR professional with a foundation of reality – what is the organisation or business function trying to achieve; how does what HR is trying to achieve fit with, bolster and assist in their achievement of that goal; and how does *how* I perform my HR role influence and impact both those situations?

The need for insight in HR

The needs and subsequent demands of leaders, teams and entire organisations can often change without warning, which can be disconcerting (not to mention frustrating) for many HR professional. The quote from Alvin Toffler above speaks of our need, in this day and age of disruption and technological evolution, to continue to learn our craft and not rest on an expectation that once an expert; always an expert. Critically, this life-long learning must happen while also recognising that the things that no longer serve us now – and into our futures – are things we must *unlearn*. Finally, the things that we may have forgotten – or forgotten to make use of – are things we must *relearn*. All of this takes insight. This insight is paired with the acknowledgement we just might need to change our approach; that the status quo isn't a great strategy for future success.

Indeed, in HR circles we borrow Marshall Goldsmith's line "What got you here, won't get you there". So true – yet most often we don't quite know what it was that got us *here*, nor what *there* looks like. HR is such as diverse profession and each day in any given role can be unlike the one before. This can result in the profession feeling like a fire-fighting role, where the practitioner goes from issue to issue in a whirlwind of busyness and being pulled in multiple directions. If this pattern persists weeks, months and even years can go by without us noticing, only to wake up one day and wonder how things got like this. We effectively stop paying attention to what's happening around us, numbed by the overwhelm of what we need to accomplish.

This also results in many practitioners losing the interest or drive they once had when they were motivated by the potential HR holds. Once they lose empathy with what's happening in their customer's world, they disengage. The HR Catalysts among us have an uncanny ability to seek, triage and make meaning out of the multitude of events and interactions that happen around them every day and remain engaged in the present yet with one eye on the future. They turn knowledge into insights that they then share with their customers, in order to help them take their part of the organisation forward. This is the first step in levelling-up your HR practice.

What does this mean in the context of the HR profession?

The HR Catalyst is continually learning; craving insights as to why situations and events occur, why people say and do what they do, and why particular outcomes eventuate. These insights are the result of learning over time; purposeful learning that morphs not stacks.

Often, we think of learning as adding to what we already know, to what we have learned before. Morphed learning, on the other hand, is when we recognise the truth has changed. Like when the realisation was made that the Earth is in fact round and not flat as was believed (this calculated discovery has been attributed to Galileo, Aristotle, Pythagoras and Eratosthenes – all of whom would have been considered outliers as they battled to convince others to literally think outside the box), this type of learning undoes what has been known before. As the (round) world of work is disrupted beyond our imaginations, what we *know* to be true in the workplace is equally being challenged. We are being forced to question everything we think we know about how work best happens. The status quo is no longer an acceptable place to defend. Catalyst HR practitioners recognise this and use it to their advantage – as you'll soon see.

What constitutes the Human Resources profession today is vastly different from what it was 15, 20 or 30 years ago. Even over the last five years, the gamut of fields and areas of influence our profession has a finger in has expanded. It is now very difficult to put a hard and fast definition of what HR actually is – partly because it's context specific. The HR Catalyst needs to know what HR actually comprises and constitutes in their own organisation, while also recognising that this will inevitably change. So, there is a need to be playful with it! Knowing the distinction between HR in your organisation versus HR in any other business allows for a more precise evaluation of ideas and initiatives espoused as 'best practice', to see if they are fit for application in one's own workplace.

The role of Interest, Attention and Empathy

Before we dive deep into the three elements of this Insight dimension, we first need to examine how HR catalysts go about developing this understanding – by showing interest, paying attention and ultimately displaying empathy.

Firstly, interest is a psychological state of engagement, experienced in the moment, and also a predisposition to engage repeatedly with particular ideas, events, or objects over time. Interest in the context of your organisation as an HR professional is fundamental in shaping how you practice. Showing a keen sense of interest in what you're trying to achieve, where your work fits into helping your customers achieve their goals and in exploring alternative pathways to success is essential in building rapport with those you work with, lead and coach. It's like using a microscope – the further you zoom in on the object, the greater the definition, and with it, your sense of awe. It's this keen interest in digging deeper into issues, uncovering alternatives and exploring options to progress that helps those around you see that you understand their situation and that you are the person they need to help them through their people-issues.

Secondly, paying attention to those you serve is the next step in developing clearer insight into what is going on in your organisation. If a keen sense of interest is the thinking aspect of insight, paying attention is the action that results from it – the doing aspect that sees your credibility grow with managers and customers alike. Think about attention as the demonstration of your interest. It takes a good listening ear, some clear open-ended questions that elicit stories and an ability to stop talking. The best HR Catalysts are those who choose when to speak and when to shut-up. In doing so, they empower and enable those they serve to open-up, increasing the catalyst's insightfulness of what's really going on.

Once interest and attention are in play, the third element of being insightful is empathy – commonly viewed as the ability to identify with or understand the perspective, experiences, or motivations of another individual. In the context of the HR profession, this requires an action – a sharing of the other person's emotional state. Without it, you just have a raised awareness. This active sharing is what differentiates the approach to empathy catalyst HR professionals practice from the everyday person's definition of empathy. It goes a step further than simply recognising another's emotions inside yourself, to turning this recognition into insights that inform your behaviour with that person.

HR Catalysts spark change in others by being interested, paying deep attention and sharing a level of empathy that makes the customer feel understood. This explains the need to take your interest and attention and turn it into feelings you can relay back to the customer. They must be able to experience that you not only understand what it's like to be them in their world, but you can also develop insights into how to improve their situation. This can be interpreted as needy if not handled delicately. But, when executed with care and an intention to serve the internal customer, displaying deep empathy for the issue, goal or situation they bring to your attention can be a real turning point in your professional relationship.

Let's now dive into the three areas of insight the HR Catalyst needs to understand.

Big picture context

HR Catalysts nest their practice in a deep foundation of knowing why their organisation exists, what it's trying to achieve and how they add value to their customers. Some even prioritise understanding how their company differentiates itself from its competitors. This is vital simply because HR sits within the bubble; not *as* the bubble – HR exists to serve the organisation in its strategic and operational pursuit of goals; not the other way around. Many HR practitioners, leaders and entire teams make the mistake of behaving as if the rest of the organisation exists to serve HR's goals and intentions. If this is you – STOP IT. NOW!

Okay, with that rant out of way, we should now have an understanding that developing some insight into what the organisation is trying to achieve is the only way for HR to demonstrate its relevance, timeliness and value-adding potential. Let's look at the key questions you could seek to answer in order to grow your understanding of how you might influence future success.

Strategic intent

What is your organisation trying to achieve? Knowing the answer to this is important, because everything HR does must progress the business towards achieving that intent. Simple. If it doesn't, you and your team should seriously question why you are doing it and if you should continue (I'd suggest you don't – I reckon you've got enough on your plate, so culling a few tasks with little meaningful payback is surely a good thing).

Key questions you need to be able to answer about your organisation and how your HR practice influences and adds value include:

What is the organisation's purpose, vision and mission?

Why are these what they are?

Do they have a clear cascading flow that links them?

If not, whom might you seek greater clarity from?

Who could you spark a conversation with to highlight any misalignment?

What are your organisation's sacred cows?

What is your organisation's status quo?

Describe the organisation's internal culture

How might an external customer describe it?

Can you outline your organisation's strategy?

Can you do so in different language that suits a varied internal audience?

What are three key facets of this strategy and why did you pick these ones?

You see, many HR practitioners are not thinking this way. You don't need to be able to answer all these questions right now, but you do need to know how and who to find the answers from, and get out from behind the desk and seek those answers. HR Catalysts spend time each day connecting with people right across their business. This is critical to stay in the game. You need to be in the know so that you can help anticipate issues and provide advice and solutions... sometimes even before your customers know they have a problem to solve. How cool is that?!

Insightful is actually less about *thinking*, and more about *doing*. You should now see that practicing HR is no longer just the HR *stuff* you know, but how that fits with the unique context of your organisation and even the specific customers you work with. This may require you to ignore or unlearn many of the things you thought you knew and may have prided yourself on – something we'll go deep on in the next chapter.

Workforce challenges

How well you know the dynamics and context within your organisation can set you up for great success as an HR Catalyst. Organisations are called such because they are a collection of smaller businesses clustered together in an organised manner (or at least, that was the original intention when the term was coined). Within each of those businesses or divisions is a set of challenges – some faced by every team, others by only a few individuals. Such challenges might include competition for attention, airtime or a seat at the table in a strategy meeting, or market-related challenges that affect only a portion of the organisation such as a scarce talent pool.

Being acutely aware of these is an ok start. Being known for being interested in learning what they are, what they mean for that particular unit and where those leaders think you can assist positions you perfectly as the go-to HR business partner. Remember – HR Catalysts spark change in others, which means you need to know where to target the ignition source of that spark.

Useful questions include:

What are all the professions your organisation employs?

Where do you source them from – industries, organisations, sectors, regions?

Which ones are changing or being disrupted right now?

What about in 18–24 months time?

What does that mean for HR in-house?

What **types** of people do you employ – how do you categorise them?

Which ones get most attention from HR? Why?

Which get the least HR attention? Why?

Depending on the industry your organisation operates in, your answers to some of the above questions will vary because of external factors outside of your control. You may have limited influence over these, but you should still be aware of them and of how they are shaping your answers, in order to provide a tailored service to the managers and teams you work with. Other answers may be personality-based or influenced by such demographic factors like education. Examine your answers and be curious with them – why did you answer this way? What's behind that?

Then there are those people who demand more attention (positive or negative) from HR than others. Some managers, some teams, even some staff simply require more of your time. Depending on your mindset, this can be a source of frustration, or an opportunity to develop a better relationship by seeking greater insight into their context.

This demand placed on HR can also be continuous or temporary and intermittent. For example, if you work in a business-partner type role, you'll no doubt have at least one manager who demands a disproportionate amount of your time than others in your portfolio. They might be known as high-maintenance, and it is generally accepted that that is how they have always been and will continue to be so. Understanding why this is and seeking answers to further questions that crop-up from seeking and developing insights is a vital skill of the HR Catalyst. Make curiosity your secret weapon.

On the other hand, you may have a customer who is undertaking a review of their team or function for the first time in their career and requires greater input from you. You know this is temporary and if you coach and advise them well, they are unlikely to require the same level of hands-on service should they undertake another review in the future. The savvy HR Catalyst works in the present to position themselves for the future.

The competition

Most HR teams and practitioners have little awareness of the external forces at play outside the organisation walls, believing that as HR is an internal function, it only needs to focus on what is happening within the org chart. If they do, it's often lip-service to what they've heard repeated by leaders of other externally facing functions who deal day-to-day with 'the outside world'. This is foolish, old-school HR that simply reinforces the status-quo. HR Catalysts are uber-Business Partners – they're savvy practitioners who are not only in touch with customer needs, but also have a good business sense about them. This isn't to say they need to have run a business, simply that they need to understand how their organisation operates. This includes knowing the market it operates in.

Consider these:

Who are your organisation's biggest competitors?

What are they best at?

What are they worse at?

What are the points of difference between your organisation and these others?

What disruptors are operating in the industry and why are they a potential threat?

Who could you discuss these topics with to get greater clarity?

Change

Yes, change is indeed constant, and it can be argued either way as to whether change is happening faster, or more, or with greater impact. The point is, do you know what change means for your organisation? Do you know the implications this has on what the work of HR is now and in the near future?

What about the personal impact that change and disruption could have or is currently having on the people you serve? The HR Catalyst leads, coaches and supports their customers to feel as if they have some sense of control over their future in times of change. Whether they embark on the change themselves or the change has been thrust upon them, a person's response to change is often not about the actual detail of the change, but more about them not being able to see themselves in that future state. HR Catalysts help people imagine their future and decide the steps needed to make that reality.

It may help to ponder these:

What are the technological changes or disruptions affecting your business right now?

How are these impacting your customers?

What might these disruptions look like in five years' time

List three major ways your organisation is changing?

What does this mean for HR?

How should HR respond?

How can you as a HR Catalyst help deliver on, speed-up, or dampen the effect of this change (as appropriate)?

HR business acumen

Once we have a deep and active appreciation for the context in which your HR practice operates, we can then focus on how to enable that context. Essentially, this is about how you create an ideal match between what the business needs and how you go about executing your role as an HR Catalyst. What is the most appropriate and optimised HR practice to do this with?

HR Business Acumen as a concept is simple, yet most often overlooked by well-meaning HR professionals. Regardless of which phase of development your organisation is at – be that start-up, growth, consolidate, restructure, level-up, you name it – the HR service delivered must be on the same page. To deliver appropriate services with a level of stretch that drives individuals, teams and entire groups of functions forward, HR Catalysts must know the lie of the land.

What is the territory within which you're playing?

When you know the terrain, you can map-out strategies that suit the landscape to ensure the tactics are at least minimally viable.

The city of Dunedin, New Zealand was largely settled by migrants from Scotland, who took the street plan of central Edinburgh and applied it to the new Dunedin site. This seems like a great plan – using the expertise they had from one project to make a second project more efficient. Unfortunately, Dunedin itself has very different geography to Edinburgh. Dunedin is based around a harbour basin, which gives it a large number of very steep streets. Edinburgh, on the other hand, was build on a flat landscape with none of these challeges. An HR Catalyst would have looked to apply a dose of reality to the situation, arguing where the original plan could be leveraged to create a better experience in the new location.

It therefore follows that one of the most important skills HR professionals need to develop is business acumen. As a species, the inquisitive nature of us humans is to ask WHY? Why are we here? Why is that important? Why should we bother? If we don't know the why of something, we don't tend to act on it. Having business acumen enables us to understand the drivers of organisational success and speak the same language as the business. Only when we in HR understand how our business makes or loses money, and what internal policies or processes influence our ability to satisfy clients, customers and stakeholders, will we be able to develop valuable insights and truly partner with the business and make an impact through exceptional HR service.

How can you ensure you've got the HR context clear before charging on? The last thing we want is to push a well-intentioned but poorly designed initiative. Work through this list of questions to check your level of insightfulness:

How does HR enable your organisation to fulfil its mission and vision?

What is the agenda, the concerns and the issues held by people across your organisation?

How does HR add value to your organisation's customers, clients and stakeholders?

How do you know this to be true? How are you responding to this knowledge?

How has HR changed in your organisation over the last five years?

How effective has this change been?

What are the HR technology pressures and changes that are influencing your team's service provision right now? What will they be in 18 months time?

What are the pressures shaping the HR profession now and over the next 3–5 years?

What about HR do you hold sacred? Why? What about your team / colleagues?

How are these positively and negatively influencing and impacting your HR practice?

The reason these questions are so important is because they ground your practice of the HR profession in local, real-time reality. There is no point being the most proficient remuneration specialist in a small start-up, or focus your attention on enhancing long-term organisational culture just before a planned merger – meet your market just ahead of where they're at.

Did you pick up on the key words in that last sentence? "Meet your market"? You need to always be thinking about your customer base as your market and how you can serve them better. You're not competing with your HR colleagues to out-do them, but to serve your customer at a level and cadence that keeps them keen to work with you; just slightly ahead of their expectations. In doing so, you might just inspire your HR teammates to up their game too!

This idea of meeting your market is often a foreign consideration for HR practitioners. Catalysts in the field have a clear vision of their market and test their insights regularly via check-ins and catch-ups with key customers within their organisation. It's important to be able to speak their language and to talk about their issues and concerns, their aspirations and hesitations in their language (as we'll see in coming chapters). For now, ensure you clearly understand how HR can impact the organisation and look to develop capability in crucial, future-focused areas that serve those needs.

Your own HR practice

Organisational context = Check.
Clarity on the internal HR capability required to that context = Check.

That leaves *your own HR Practice* as the third element of the *Insightful* dimension that guides HR Catalysts to success. This is where the rubber hits the road in terms of knowing what you bring to the profession and your workplace.

It starts with knowing yourself better. For a start, not knowing yourself well means you miss opportunities for development, which can mean you quickly become redundant and not useful in the mind of a customer. HR Catalysts know themselves well. Their self-awareness allows them operate at a similar level as their customers. Knowing their strengths allows them to create and leverage opportunities to use those strengths. Knowing weaknesses not only makes targeting quick development easy, but also ensures the practitioner doesn't set themselves up to fail by walking into situations where they may be caught out. Some of this will be intuitive; other aspects you'll need some assistance with. Remember, the HR Catalyst is a seeker who thrives in gathering actionable knowledge. Feedback is your ally, though as we'll see in the next chapter, not all feedback is useful.

How can you know if you know yourself well enough? Seek answers to these:

How would you describe your own HR practice?

How would your customer managers and colleagues describe it?

What are you known for in your organisation? Is this what you want to be known for?

In what ways do you practice HR differently from others on your team or in your HR network?

How accessible and easy are you to work with?

What feedback are you seeking out right now? Why?

What preferences do you have around types of HR work?

What work lights you up and turns you off?

Where do you fit in HR's enabling of the organisation's strategy?

Is this where you're best placed to add value? How could you add further value?

How can you position HR better in your organisation?

What are you known for? Is that helpful to both your practice and your organisation?

Brand YOU

Essentially, these questions seek to uncover your *brand* of HR practice. HR professionals are often well-versed in the concepts of employment branding and EVP, but often don't consider their own brand of HR. What do people at work think about when they see your number appear on their phone or your avatar on the intranet or messaging app? Knowing the truth people hold about you is vital for your future success. The perceptions people hold dictate their behaviour with you – some people will have you completely wrong. Do you know who they are and what they think? What could you do to change their perceptions?

We will touch on this concept of your brand of HR throughout the remainder of this book, but it's worth having this concept in the back of your mind as you continue to read. Fundamentally, whether or not you have thought about your HR brand before, you definitely already have one. This isn't an attempt to make you paranoid, just an important aspect to keep in mind. After all, you have complete ability to influence what people think of you in the next interaction you have with them – what might you do differently or reinforce? What do you want them to remember about you in that interaction?

The HR Catalyst is deliberate and careful about the brand they display. Gathering insights about what this brand is, and what you want it to be, is a solid place to start.

CHAPTER TWO

Unattached

BE	DO	HAVE
Insightful	Understand	Greater Empathy
Unattached	Surrender	Deeper Wisdom
Focused	Hustle	Meaningful Progress
Connected	Collaborate	Stronger Connection
Yourself	Believe	True Presence

Unattached

> "Letting things go is an act of far greater power than defending or hanging on"
>
> – Eckhart Tolle

In chapter one we explored the need for HR professionals to develop insights into the context in which they are being a people and culture professional. HR Catalysts get this 100% and as a result are able to fully serve their customer managers and operate above their peers. However, simply adding greater knowledge and meaning can be like hiking with your pack half-filled with equipment you don't necessarily need, or even worse, with rocks. The new understanding – the stuff you do need – is often piled on top of this stuff you no longer need, stuff that's completely useless and weighing you down. The next action of an HR Catalyst priming themselves for greater impact is to empty the pack of unnecessary equipment and weight. In some cases, this is knowledge you no longer need because the tasks you perform don't require you to keep up a skill from the past. In others, it could be an experience you haven't let go of that is fundamentally holding you back from future greatness. The former can be dealt with quickly through prioritisation. The baggage of the past needs to be worked through with more patience and acceptance. Fundamentally, the HR Catalyst practices non-attachment throughout their practice. Being *unattached* (which is not quite the same as detached) is the second dimension of the HR Catalyst model.

We all have some degree of baggage. I'm sure, reading this, you can bring to mind something you're holding on to that doesn't serve your ability to be better or more effective in the future. It's a part of being human. It's likely we're the only species on earth that truly carries around emotions tied to past experiences. Pets learn lessons; people make stories out of them. Then we relive these narratives over and over! Your pet cat might sulk around the house the week you return from holiday, but that never resurfaces unconnected to your absence – each sulk is related to a recent experience. People certainly do this too, but we also retain each experience and file it away in its own distinct folder in our hearts and minds. This we carry around with us for life, ready to resurface when we allow it to. Until, that is, we let it go.

It's not all bad experiences, either. Many of our positive experiences boost our egos, such as feedback in performance appraisals or comments in meetings about a job well done from someone you didn't expect to notice. Yet, some positive experiences or feedback aren't useful. Insisting after a successful interaction that you're so good that you don't need to do further work, taking an experience of being 'right' to the extreme of believing you're 'always right' – these are examples where hanging onto too much self-worth is actual a block on the road to improvement. Recognising the difference between types of baggage and dealing with them appropriately is a key characteristic of a Catalyst HR practitioner.

These are all requisite skills on the way to levelling up your practice. Knowing what is important versus urgent; how to deal with busyness and overwhelm; seeking, hearing and triaging feedback so the important stuff 'sticks' and being able to set aside that which isn't; being clear on what might be holding your own HR practice back – all these things are vital for you to gain the clarity required to focus on where to spend your energy at work.

When considering your ability to practice unattachment to the stuff that might be holding you back, the Catalyst HR model considers three key elements. Your ability to:

1. Know what matters
2. Prioritise and decide with absolute clarity
3. Move on from what's holding you back

Knowing what matters

Often when we prioritise tasks, we look at them in terms of what we can delay, delegate or do now. But there's a step before this decision phase. The term *decide* essentially means to cut-off or eliminate choice. It has similar origins to pesticide and genocide, where the goal is to eliminate the unwanted. So, the focus here is to understand what matters, what to focus attention and energy on, where to turn and who to listen to. It's not about dividing up an already over-flowing task list. It's not about adding more to your task list, in fact it's the complete opposite. It's time to home-in on what matters by cutting out that which doesn't help you in your mission to become an HR Catalyst.

Let's be clear: Being a Catalyst HR practitioner is not a matter of sitting back and waiting for people to let you know how you're getting on – you need to be proactive. It's also not about getting feedback only from the usual suspects, like your manager and immediate colleagues. HR Catalysts are seekers of knowledge – not just about their profession, but how they go about implementing that expertise. The HR Catalyst model is one of behaviour; not technical skill. Thus, it's imperative you seek a wide and varied range of feedback from an equally diverse range of relevant people (note the term *relevant* – any old comment about you from someone who cannot meaningfully comment on your HR practice is just ego stroking; not feedback). Regardless of the nature, type and quality of feedback they seek out and/or receive, the HR Catalyst remains unattached to it. In their world view, and while the work is vitally important to achieving success, that success is not theirs to own or become attached to. Everything the Catalyst HR practitioner does is in service to their customers and the organisation.

Yet, it is still important to gain insight into and track your performance. Sometimes the best feedback comes from those you have clashed with in the recent past. Where have you disagreed and about what? It's how others receive you in these times that can be the greatest spark for self-change. What did they appreciate about your behaviour in hindsight, and what still irks them? This provides two exceptional opportunities – firstly, for you to gain valuable insights into how you can deal with tricky customers and situations in the future, and secondly to show your personal brand of HR practice to the eyes of an influential customer and turn that relationship around. Many HR Catalysts I've worked with have spoken of how their trickiest customer turned out to be their greatest ally, after they proactively sought to understand the sticking point in their relationship. In many instances it was a past interaction that the manager or stakeholder themselves couldn't let go of. Often it's simply a case of misunderstanding or misinterpretation. In any case, the Dalai Lama is quoted as having said "I love feedback – it tells me so much about the other person". It's useful to contemplate, but not become attached to.

Some feedback is not important or useful *right now*. Remember, we're looking for useful information about your practice that is immediately implementable or able to be turned into something useful that has impact in your work right now. At times, we get positive feedback that we interpret as us needing to keep doing 'that thing, that particular way', whether in an attitude towards work, or an approach we take with certain individuals. However, we need to be careful not to dwell on that feedback and inadvertently apply the same approach in a different setting. HR Catalysts don't apply generic, vanilla solutions (especially with people) or take a one-size-fits-all approach. To do so would be imitating what many HR practitioners are unfortunately known for i.e. not applying a customer-centric approach of empathising with the individual and meeting them where they're at.

So, what does matter for HR Catalysts to understand, work through and add to their arsenal? Actually, that's up to you and depends on your stage of career and your focus for the coming 6-18 months. It's not for me to tell you *what* matters, but for you to understand that some things *don't matter*. Be sure not to focus time and energy on those things. Your aim is to create a smaller – but more vital – bucket of characteristics that define you and your HR practice for you to work on.

Key questions for you at this part of the journey are to ask yourself:

Why do you choose to work in HR?

What do you need to learn, unlearn and/or relearn?

What assumptions and presumptions do you have about your future in the HR profession?

What feedback do you usually seek out? Why that?

What HR actions and tasks are better done by others and not by you? Why?

What might be staring you in the face that you don't notice or have been ignoring?

How do you triage information?

What are your HR truths?

What does an HR Catalyst look like in your organisation?

Who are your HR mentors and gurus?

What do you want to focus on in the coming year?

Why is that important – what is the impact or change you would see from taking action in this area?

Prioritising - deciding with clarity

As an HR practitioner, you'll be acutely aware of the need to make defensible decisions in the face of competing opinions. While your actions need to be squeaky-clean, the HR Catalyst is not so much concerned with covering their butt, but making the best decision for the situation. This means acknowledging that what best suited a situation in the past does not necessarily mean that same solution or approach remains the best for the current situation. Alvin Toffler's quote at the start of chapter 1 springs to mind – the ability to learn, unlearn and relearn. Some knowledge and skills no longer serve us, so they must be let go. Being unattached makes this easier.

In terms of your behaviour, it's useful to assess how you currently go about making decisions. What do you place importance on and why? Be careful not to fall into the trap of thinking you don't make decisions just because you're not aware of them. What is vital for the HR Catalyst is that you make clear decisions confidently – there is no point making a decision and if you then question or re-litigate what you decided. You'll be aware of how frustrating it is when executive teams decide on a course of action, only to revisit it at the first sign of opposition. Yes, you need to be flexible, but you also need to decide with clarity and conviction (which results in confident decisions making) and then move on to getting stuff done.

Fundamentally, HR Catalysts are able to wade through the to-do list and piles of busyness, quickly assessing the priority actions. Ironically, the term 'priority' itself means *the one thing*, so the fact that we use it as a plural is a bit silly. Catalysts choose one to three things to focus on and go deep with those. Having understood the imperative involved with these things, they have triaged all the rest of the busyness into things that can wait, be removed or delegated to someone else. Those tasks they select to work on are the most important in taking the organisation – or a key part of it – closer to their strategic outcomes. They do this while other not-so-savvy members of their team work endless hours running around like headless chickens, unthinkingly positioning their personal HR brands as disorganised, stressed and without expertise in the minds. Catalysts do not spread themselves too thinly trying to do too much for too many people. If this is how you work, stop and assess your task list against what really matters. Choose only one thing and go deep on that today.

Key things to think about regarding your prioritising include:

How do you currently make important decisions? Does that work for you?

List your main time-tasks. How do you weight their importance? What can you change?

What can you say 'no' to in your workplace, workday and HR practice?

What are you currently doing in your day that doesn't add value or result in progress?

What do people see you doing when you are (a) busy, (b) stressed, (c) productive?

What might this mean for your HR brand?

What about you are you going to focus on this week?

What about you are you going to amply and what are you going dial-down this month?

How will you start this process?

Moving on

As mentioned earlier in this chapter, we all have baggage – events in our past that we dwell on or use (consciously or unconsciously) to hold us back from future success. These events can be as trivial as how a team member responded to your idea in a meeting! Some of this is in our control, like how we choose to respond to feedback when it's given. Some of it we cannot control, such as how a colleague was treated during a restructuring. Some baggage we create and keep as a safety net that we like to fall back on... giving us an excuse for not pushing ourselves further or taking a risk.

HR Catalysts have a much-admired ability to move on from events; taking the positives with them and not letting any negative aspects of a situation hinder future forward-moving progress. This is a real quality many HR practitioners have trouble accomplishing. In fact, this is part of the reason HR people fail to build credibility in their practice.

The potential conflict inherent in HR's advice and practice

The people and culture profession has potential to be one of the most conflicted of all corporate roles. We deal with behaviour in addition to policy, process and practice. Most other corporate support professions striving to be strategic business partners have the luxury of dictating how others should complete a task. At the risk of insulting many in Finance, IT, and other corporate functions, they may be able to get away with a low-level of "Do as we say, not as we do". But HR is on display to portray the persona we advocate for – we must act according to a "Do as we do" system. HR teams and practitioners who fail to do this also fail to gain traction with any change they're trying to implement, due to a grave lack of trust.

We often hear managers wishing their staff could leave their personalities at the door. Yet the HR profession advocates for the need to bring your whole-self to work in order to be the best version of you. How are we meant to know which instruction to follow?! Well, it's both an easy and a hard answer. HR Catalysts do both – they recognise what it is about them they should bring to work (both personal and professional) and amplify that, while also minimising the impact of any current tendencies that don't serve their HR practice. Ultimately, they are maximising their ability to work effectively with others across the organisation.

As you go about seeking feedback on your brand of HR and how people receive you, a useful task for you to complete may be to look at where that behaviour comes from. Often we think we know where our behaviour stems from; probably in more cases we are unaware of its origins. Sometimes we are blocking out that which we don't want to accept in a state of denial. Exploring these aspects of our personality may be the secret to uncovering, unlocking and unleashing the HR Catalyst within.

Let me be clear – this is less about counselling and more about recognising what in our past influences our present. If we do not harness or deal with our past it will likely continue to influence our future HR practice. We are a product of our past, but our future is wide open. This book is about making your future in the people profession an optimal experience for you and your customers by being the best version of yourself from today onwards. With that in mind:

What are the themes in your life timeline?

What baggage are you holding on to that isn't serving your HR practice?

Who could you ask to answer this question for you honestly?

What barriers hold you back from leaning into more responsibility?

What do you need to deal with in order to be 100% in?

What feedback have you had that wasn't useful – positive or negative?

At this point, your ability to operate as an HR Catalyst rests on your proactive responses to these questions. Before moving on to chapter 3, take some time to work through the questions in this segment. But be careful to not stall progress – keep active in your understanding and triage what you can surrender quickly. Other elements about you will be a work-in-progress; maintaining a rate of progress is critical. You don't want to stall or use some inner contemplation as an excuse to not improve your practice. Afterall, you're developing into a savvy HR Catalyst.

A note on process - The need for Awareness, Acceptance, Action

Unattachment is a process – one that requires first *Awareness* of what is in the way or holding you back, then *Acceptance* of this (because feedback is great, but if you don't accept that feedback the information is largely pointless). Thirdly, you need to take *Action* in response to any new awareness, in place of becoming attached to it. This process has been the foundation of many approaches to development – from self-development in therapy, to more recently being used as a basis for some approaches to mindfulness training. In the Human Resources profession, it was popularised by

Lombardo and Eichinger in the early 2000s as an underlying principle to develop leadership competencies in support of their *Lominger* competency framework. The approach has merit in developing HR practitioners, especially given we all have things about us – knowledge, experiences, traits and characteristics – that are potentially hindering our ability to perform with greater impact, affect and/or efficiency. Practicing unattachment to these things removes the burden of dwelling-on and procrastinating, and makes taking action easier.

Awareness

Some of the questions posed for you to consider in this chapter have been about you seeking further information, building on the *Insightful* dimension of the previous chapter. Gaining an awareness of the areas you need to develop your practice enables you to zero-in on what matters. You simply need to be proactive, but not annoying. HR Catalysts seek out feedback, but in the context of how they can add further value in their work. This means you need to have regular conversations with a wide range of colleagues and collaborators in your network – both inside and outside your organisation. Raising your awareness of how you operate in the view of others can be pivoting in unlocking potential in yourself.

Acceptance

We accept the stuff we can make sense of – the information we can understand. Accepting all the feedback you gain in your role isn't the expectation here. Again, some of it is not useful; it's simply someone else's perspective. You need to triage that which is useful, and that which doesn't serve you now. It is the stuff you'll use that you need to look deeper into so you can accept what has been said. This needs to be done quickly, so you don't dwell on the content or implications – is it valuable to me practicing HR better? If not, let it go and move on to something that will see you operate better.

In addition, regardless of our response to it, we should practice acceptance of the very fact that a piece of feedback came about. It happened, so there is some learning and recognition required. Whether you agree with that piece of feedback or not is almost not the point; you can accept that there's something to learn from it without carrying the burden of taking everyone else's opinions as correct. Then move on. Maybe that will serve you at some later date. The point is to not dwell on it or use disliked feedback as an excuse for not taking action.

Action

In chapter 3 we'll really get into this process of taking action through adding some hustle into the work you undertake. But for now, it's important that the good work you've done – in gaining greater awareness of what's holding you back and accepting the need to do something about it – turns into exactly that – meaningful action. You need to be getting something done as a result. That action needs to be simple, immediate and have consequences if not undertaken. You're accountable for your impact, which means you need to get going with some focus.

CHAPTER THREE

Focused

BE	DO	HAVE
Insightful	Understand	Greater Empathy
Unattached	Surrender	Deeper Wisdom
Focused	Hustle	Meaningful Progress
Connected	Collaborate	Stronger Connection
Yourself	Believe	True Presence

Focused

> "When walking, walk. When eating, eat."
>
> – Zen Proverb

So far, we've covered the HR Catalyst's need to be insightful of their brand of HR and the context in which they operate, and the requirement for them to be unattached to whatever may be holding them back from greater impact. These two dimensions of practice both set-up and clear the way for the third dimension we now move into – that of gaining *focus* in the work you're doing as a go-getting people practitioner.

Being focused is all about getting stuff done. It's the hustle of the HR world. It needs to happen quickly and with regard to the HR Catalyst's practice of the profession, it needs to result in meaningful progress. This cannot be fully achieved without first having greater empathy for your customer's context (as we now know it) and having surrendered potential shackles. Once we know what needs doing and have moved on from potential barriers, we are ideally placed to grab opportunities with both hands. It's time to gain traction with the work ahead.

This dimension is like keeping your mind on proper rock-climbing technique. To climb efficiently, you need to put effort into your legs. It takes constant self-reminders to use the right technique here. It's all too easy to look at all the options above, predominantly pull from handholds, and burnout your arms. You need to keep your mind on the best way to do things, not the most obvious. Continuing the rock-climbing analogy, mindset and state management are vital to a successful climb. It would be unfortunate to lose your nerve on a rock-face dozens of metres off the ground. Likewise, HR

Catalysts must hold their nerve in the face of challenging themselves. This is less about putting on a brave face and more about setting yourself up for success by learning to manage your state of being in all manner of situations.

In any realm, focus requires persistence, as well as the need to form productive habits. In this chapter we will explore the need for the HR Catalyst to develop habits that reinforce the brand of HR you want to be known for, while amplifying your impact. In particular, this *Focused* dimension requires four distinct areas for the HR Catalyst:

1. Relentless forward progress
2. Leading and coaching
3. Influencing those who matter
4. Accountability

Relentless forward progress

Persistence and tenacity are noble characteristics that have been held in high regard for centuries. They are also qualities of the HR Catalyst, but they do come with a proviso: stubbornness and an impulse to 'flog a dead horse' are not sensible (or sustainable) approaches for HR Catalysts to take to their work. Indeed, making relentless forward progress is more an outcome of the practitioner's behaviour; not the behaviour itself. The savvy practitioner knows when to stop and take stock of a situation. If a process or project is clearly not gaining traction or making progress, there's no point forcing it. Instead, they know how to quickly assess the situation (be insightful) and decide on a new course of action (be unattached to the old process).

The role of habits in Focus

Forming positive habits around your HR practice is vital to achieving a sense of progress. James Clear, author of *Atomic Habits*, notes how small habits can have a surprisingly powerful impact on your life. He likens their impact to a pilot changing course just a couple of degrees. The nose of the plane would move only a couple of feet, with nobody on board noticing a thing, but over the course of a flight from one side of the United States to the other, the plane would be several hundred miles off course. We don't notice these changes because their immediate impact is negligible, but the HR Catalyst looks to make habits that have a significant return.

Such a habit might be based on incredible customer service, such as scheduling regular times to meet your client and checking-in to see what works best for them. You might ask, at an initial meeting, if it is ok to record the conversation on your phone so you can be fully present and not have to take notes. Even better if you send the recording to the manager when you follow-up after the meeting, including having already completed some of the tasks you committed to.

Forming habits that stick requires a process of first needing a cue, which triggers a response (when repeated becomes a routine), which in turn is followed by a reward. James Clear explains how humans are motivated by the anticipation of the reward rather than the reward itself. We can't rely on some far-away future goal to keep us motivated in the present. Therefore, making the habit itself attractive is a secret to successfully implementing behaviours that drive progress forward.

When trying to build focus as a habit, we also need to be careful our efforts don't get derailed by people or processes pushing our buttons. HR Catalysts are mindful that there will always be some level of interference, a fly in the ointment. These can be characterised as either *Tensions*, *Triggers* or *Trolls*. It's worth understanding the difference between each, being prepared with some strategies to handle them, and understanding how a shift in your perspective can actually reduce the number of issues you come into contact with.

Tensions comprise the environment in which you work. It could be issues with the culture, the vibe about the place, or the teams within which you are required to operate. I suspect you're well familiar with how these kind of external tensions feel! Not all of these negative environmental factors are widely known however, as many are aspects of the internal environment that affect your ability to practice HR. Some of these tensions may be within yourself – judgements, preconceptions and assumptions you have made that are either unresolved or have recently been highlighted as unhelpful. In which case, you must seek to understand these better and surrender what doesn't serve you.

It's important to recognise at this point that not all tension is negative. Focused HR Catalysts recognise that a level of tension is positive in motivating individuals to do hustle and do better. Tension raises levels of alertness and awareness; both are helpful in engaging robust debate. Just as in one extreme we come up against tension that cripples you with stress and indecision, without any tension at all we don't tend to be challenged nor incentivised to improve things. It's simply about finding the balance and having the right amount of tension to keep you alert.

Triggers are the aspects of work that either set you up or set you off. Again, like tensions, they can be positive or negative towards your ability to make progress. Triggers reside within you – they are a mindset that has the ability to bolster your self-assurance or tear-down your self-confidence in a matter of words. HR Catalysts master their triggers by surrounding themselves with people and interactions that positively reinforce their values, while steering clear of those that are filled with toxic energy. Obviously negative situations cannot be avoided all the time – this is HR after all, and people behave badly, and it may be your role to deal with such people and scenarios. However, astute HR practitioners have a knack for depersonalising the toxic nature of work and treating work as a game.

Finally, *Trolls* are those people who bring you down – either intentionally or inadvertently. The internet is rife with trolls, and so too is the workplace... if you let people get to you. Again, the HR Catalysts among us surround themselves whenever possible with people who build them up, rather than pull them down. However, a big part of dealing with trolls is giving them the chance to not exist in the first place. You'd be horrified at how many 'difficult relationships' are actually a result of our own misunderstandings, assumptions, and failure to communicate. An HR Catalyst doesn't make assumptions about a person, they find out what's going on and if they can help. Do this well, and you'll find that the number of real trolls in your life is greatly reduced.

A response to Tensions, Triggers and Trolls in your working life is to practice the art of being Anti-Fragile, a concept coined by Nicholas Nasim Taleb in his book of the same name. Pointing out the term 'Fragile' has no opposite in the English language, Taleb wrote about the concept of Anti-Fragility being things that gain from disorder. Traditionally, we consider the opposite of fragile to be strong and hardy, but such strength often means things are brittle. Anti-fragility means something that genuinely profits or benefits from chaos or stress.

This is a useful concept for HR Catalysts to consider. It is similar to the old expression *what doesn't kill you makes you stronger*. So, at this point, it is useful to ask yourself some more questions around your ability to relentless progress forward:

How are you practicing in an anti-fragile manner?

What is your chaos? Is it real or perceived?

What are your tensions, triggers and trolls at work?

Describe your resilient characteristics and traits.

How does your team handle tension, debate and disagreement?

Unpack a project that has stalled – what are your two critical next moves?

What's preventing you from gaining further traction in your HR practice?

Leading and coaching

A fundamental premise of the Catalyst model is that HR (and the wider people profession) is a key leadership role in any organisation. Those practicing HR should keep this as a practicing philosophy and use it to triage not only the work undertaken, but also the impact you strive to make.

Leadership is a service role and in HR's case this is about creating environments for people to thrive, to be the best versions of themselves and for the organisation to benefit as best it can from having its people engaged in meaningful work. Everything HR does must take the organisation closer to achieving its desired goals. Are we leading the organisation forward with the work we do? Did you lead HR in service of the organisation today? As a result of the work HR does, is the organisation in a better place today than it was this time last week? At times it can be hard to pinpoint immediate benefit from HR, as transformation takes time. It is not HR's role to do the leading for leaders; it's HR's role to best enable leaders to lead.

It would be unfortunate to read the above paragraphs and think I'm referring to HR leaders – only those in management roles within the professional. The type of leadership I'm referring to is actually about people leaders, program leaders and change leaders. Delegated authority is not vital for you to lead others, but HR in a sense has delegated that authority by its very nature. The expectation is that HR and all of us practitioners lead the better utilisation of people and their experience of work. The most junior HR staff member can provide leadership of a process and advice to the most senior manager in the business – what matters is how you are being in that moment. How we go about our work of HR allows us to gain greater traction with customers and projects more than the what it is we do.

HR Catalysts take the lead on key projects – there is definitely a need for fundamental project management skills in the Catalyst's portfolio of skills. Yet traditional project management has been very task and checklist oriented. The HR Catalyst leads projects by empowering others to shoulder the load and thus put new skills into practice. For sure, you will roll up your sleeves and get your hands dirty in the work that needs to be done, but the leadership approach of a HR Catalyst is one where others are empowered and enabled to stretch themselves. Afterall, you'll likely have multiple projects on the go.

But project leadership is not the extent of the work of the Catalyst, and it's here we might have to start developing new skills. Your core skill to develop is your ability to coach others: leaders and staff at all levels. Coaching involves asking great questions. The best coaches do not provide many answers at all, but rather are great conversationalists who ask the type of questions that elicit a train of thought that sees the person being coached come up with their own answers. Questions that make your customers think about the impact of their actions, the potential for success and what that looks like for their staff, questions that require managers to imagine alternative scenarios and see their people in a different reality, these are gold for HR Catalysts to gain greater traction.

The beauty of the HR Catalyst as a coach is that you do not need to be an expert in the topic you are coaching a customer through (which you would if you were mentoring them, as a mentoring relationship is one where the mentor has 'been-there-and-done-that. This is not the case with coaching). You simply need to be an expert at asking great questions that make people think. The only way to get better is to …. Well, ask more questions! The deeper you go, the more effective you are, but be careful – it's a fine line and many go too far. This is why HR Catalysts also use their emotional intelligence and self-awareness to great effect.

Coaching effectively takes a good deal of rapport and a solid relationship, which we'll dive into in the next chapter, but for now consider:

Expand on this statement: "HR is primarily a leadership function because ...."

How can HR amplify its leadership role in your organisation?

How are you leading HR practice in your organisation?

What is different about your HR leadership? How do you know it's effective?

Do you use coaching as a key tool to spark change in others? How?

Is this part of your HR brand (i.e. would others around you describe you this way)?

Influencing those who matter

HR Catalysts operate on the premise that they get work done *through* people; not by doing more themselves. To be fair, the HR Catalysts I know and have trained are incredibly hard working and diligent. They're also smart, savvy workers who use the people around them to get things done – they influence those who matter.

First, they have the credibility to influence, which comes from how well others can relate to you. I call this your *Relatability Quotient* (RQ) – the measure of how well others can relate to you, plus your ability to make good use of that level of relatability.

RQ will get you a long way in your HR career. You'll no doubt be aware that organisations are often run by personalities.

Some people climb the ladder, while others (perhaps equally as deserving) do not. It's about who you know and who knows you. Note that it's also understandable if, while reading that last point, you recoil and think to yourself "It's HR's role to ensure proper process is followed so this doesn't happen!" Well, yes and no – HR's role is certainly to champion fairness, but HR Catalysts are under no delusions that a few strong personalities don't have influence that outstrips their formal authority. The key takeaway for you here is that it's your role to figure out ways to (a) get on their radar, and (b) influence these people to achieve better outcomes for the organisation – i.e. get done what you need done. This may mean they take the credit. Let that go.

Second, you need to know who matters. The people you need to relate better to, to influence at a higher, more effective level, and who you can work with and through to make stuff happen, are pivotal in creating opportunities you can really invest yourself in and get some great work done. Let's be clear; a selfish desire to have a great experience at work as an HR Catalyst does not need to detract from your ability to provide world-class customer service and deliver unbelievable results. So, to create a list of influencers in your organisation and what you know about them – their skills, interests, experiences and aspirations – and tag these alongside projects and initiatives you plan to undertake in the coming months, would be a great move. Again, effectiveness here comes down to the relationship you develop with key individuals and spending value-add time with them.

Your RQ, and knowing who matters across your organisation, are important things for you to think about:

What is your Relatability Quotient?

Who matters in your HR practice? Why? Why them?

How and where could you generate a little _more_ friction in your practice?

How could you do this in your team and your organisation?

How easy are you to work with? What do your key customers say?

Accountability

At this point we're about halfway through the Catalyst HR model, and it may seem odd that accountability only now gets a mention. It's a critical characteristic of operating as someone who sparks change in others across your organisation. It's also something that HR as a profession is not necessarily known for, despite a focus on ensuring *others* are held accountable through performance management frameworks. Yet, we needed to lay the foundations of being Insightful and Unattached, or else we would have been holding ourselves accountable to an unattainable and unfiltered amount of work.

Being accountable as an HR Catalyst requires three fundamental opportunities you must take (or create) for yourself:

1. Standing up
2. Stepping in
3. Standing out

Standing up is about exactly that; taking a stand for something. It's about having an opinion and standing by it.

Putting yourself out there and being prepared to take some flack for the view you have. It's not about being a dick, or disagreeing for the sake of having your voice heard, but it is about putting your hand-up and being counted. This is the first move of HR accountability – have an opinion. Too many HR practitioners are caught up in pleasing people and saying "yes" to everything, then they wonder why they are not invited to the table. Even if your opinion rubs some people up the wrong way, you're better to have had your say than to shrink into the background and remain silent.

Of course, you need to pick your moments, but if they don't arise then you need to create moments that serve your purpose by *Stepping in*. HR Catalysts who step in to situations, problems, projects and situations, particularly ones that other shy-away from, create moments and opportunities to not only make a real difference, but to change the brand of HR in organisations and even industries. There's a knack to identifying situations that will allow you to leverage your skills versus ones that will see you sink. You need to be able to read the situation well enough to pick your moment, but not dwell too long so that the moment passes. That's called procrastinating into inaction! Stepping in to tricky situations takes courage, but you can receive a huge payback for your efforts. It's in these situations that you stand out from the pack.

HR as a profession is not one known for *Standing out* from the crowd. It has for decades been known merely as the place that gives out hugs and comes down hard on behaviour that discriminates. It's ironic that HR is also widely known as having a "Do as we say, not as we do" attitude. As a profession HR often stands out for all the wrong reasons, not least because you can easily find the following examples of HR acting contrary to the best practice it preaches:

HR advising working around issues rather than addressing what's pressing.

HR getting involved in office politics and seeming more concerned with hierarchy.

HR (rightly or wrongly) failing to be transparent with process and progress.

HR people ironically having trouble seeing the human side of issues.

HR being subjective, rather than objective, and taking sides.

So, the time is ripe for the HR Catalysts among us to take a stand; to stand for making change in our organisations as well as in how HR is practiced. Standing up for a challenge and a position that may not be popular can one of the hardest steps to take in your career, but also the most rewarding.

Have you been standing up, stepping in and standing out in your HR practice? Ask yourselves these questions to take a benchmark of where you are now:

What does 'standing up', 'stepping in' and 'standing out' look like in your HR practice?

What would each of these fundamental opportunities look like for you?

Where in your work could you take on a little more pressure?

Where in your team could you create and/or apply a little more pressure?

How do people you work with describe your ability to get stuff done?

How does your HR practice challenge the status quo?

A note on the HR Catalyst embracing HR digitalisation

Recent research by Gartner defined digitalisation as *the deployment of digital technologies and practices to enhance existing business models or to create new business and/or operating models.* This same research found over two-thirds of business leaders believe their companies will no longer be competitive if they do not become significantly more digitalised by 2020. The clock is therefore well and truly ticking, and HR must be at the forefront leading this uptake and leveraging of new technologies.

In our own profession, HR leaders have cited digitalising HR as their number one priority, because of its expected impact of employee experience. Following on from our discussion in chapter 1 about understanding the role of HR, digitalisation of the profession will only work if we adopt a catalyst mindset; one that moves from user-centric to consumer-centric. What do staff value in their experience of work that assists them to add more value in their work?

HR Catalysts don't wait for change to happen

Futurist Dave Wild believes, contrary to common opinion, that change isn't happening faster, we're just reacting slower to the changes around us as the amount of change increases. He advocates (rightly so, in my opinion) that the change we see today was set in play a decade ago – what we experience now was largely determined in our past. So, what does this mean for the practice of HR? What will be the impact of traditional job disintegration be on HR? The Catalysts among us aren't waiting – they're already creating their future.

It's widely accepted that whole jobs are unlikely to be replaced by robotics and AI. Instead, large components of roles will be automated, requiring a partial 'plugging of gaps' required across organisations. The same will occur in HR. Have you thought about where? Have you thought about how you can leverage this coming change, instead of being waylaid by it?

The adaptive HR professional – gaining traction in change

For decades the Human Resources profession has constantly rebuilt itself on the foundations of the drive for greater employee productivity depending on the industrial imperatives of the day. Over the past 20 years HR has moved from an enforcer of rules and policy, through a transition from staff satisfaction to engagement. Now, with a global move away from traditional, full-time employment as the predominant workforce model, the relationship between employee and employer is morphing again. So much so that today the tenets of 'loyalty' and 'engagement' are fading in significance and HR is turning towards the next big thing. Indeed, many believe we have landed on it – it's known as the Employee Experience.

The thing is, whether employee experience is or isn't the next step-change in HR thinking doesn't matter. What is important is that HR continues to evolve. It's the role of the HR Catalysts to steer this evolution and gain traction with and through change. We cannot avoid change – indeed, this is how the HR profession has remained relevant. The HR Catalyst is at the forefront of the next evolution of the people profession as these practitioners are not only technically savvy, but drive change through how they practice.

CHAPTER FOUR

Connected

BE	DO	HAVE
Insightful	Understand	Greater Empathy
Unattached	Surrender	Deeper Wisdom
Focused	Hustle	Meaningful Progress
Connected	Collaborate	Stronger Connection
Yourself	Believe	True Presence

Connected

> *"Even the Lone Ranger didn't do it alone."*
>
> – Anon

Parts of your organisation may not seem all that organised at times. Perhaps they feel chaotic, hectic, frenetic, maybe even shambolic and in disarray. Maybe they are, or maybe it's just perception. Maybe they started stable, but are now undergoing intense change. Regardless, organisations become disorganised due to one thing and one thing only. People.

It's not technology, systems, processes or even market influences than cause chaos. People cause the chaos and it's only people that experience chaos. Yet, this is also what makes each and every organisation unique and full of boundless potential. People create and destroy company cultures. They work together, compete and require intervention. They create, conspire and complain. The beauty of this is that every team that exists is not replicated anywhere else on the planet. More so, that dynamic of experience and potential, aspiration and inspiration, will never be the same once one member leaves and is 'replaced' by someone else. Indeed, a team changed never returns to its original form – nor should it.

The glue that holds all this together is *Connection*. With stronger, deeper, more trust-based working collaboration, organisations can withstand turbulent times and the angst and tension thrown-up by disruption. So too can the HR Catalyst.

In this chapter we canvas the need for you, as a practitioner who sparks change in others, to form the best possible connection with those who matter. It is this collaboration that will help transform your organisation towards its goals. The three elements of this dimension comprise:

1. **Build networks**
2. **Maintain relationships**
3. **Have better conversations**

Build networks

Your ability to connect with those you need to work better with now and into the future is a critical focus area for you to practice. The key here is that it's not the process of networking that makes an HR catalyst, but rather the strength of the network that has been built. As Janine Garner puts it in her 2017 book *It's Who You Know: how a network of 12 people can fast-track your success*, sure networking matters; but your network matters more!

What she means by this is that opportunities come to those who are known by others for knowing something. Those in your immediate network must know you more than the veneer, superficial level that social media thrives on. It does not matter whether distant *others* are aware you exist – awareness must be meaningful and result in benefits to you both to be of value. It's your network across your organisation and the wider HR community who will not only make your ability to affect change easier, but also create a ripple effect through those that matter. This is how you amplify your impact and credibility.

Garner suggests moving from *transactional* to *transformational* networking. This takes a level of curiosity above simply being interested in people. It's a mindset that drives the HR Catalyst to seek more information than is offered. Above all, and remembering that HR is a service role, Catalyst HR practitioners need to adopt a mindset of attention-out by asking "How can I serve this person?" It's adopting this mindset and taking actions to serve your network that will see you become known for adding value to others.

So, how do you know who to connect with?

Garner recommends asking yourself the following questions in a sequence of sorting, searching, seeking and sinking your network, adapted below. This echoes the earlier chapters of *Understanding* who your network is – who's in your organisation that can potentially become key to your progress? Then we need to think about *Surrendering* – what assumptions have you made about people that are limiting your ability to connect with them? Even deeper, who have you written-off because of past interactions or experiences with that person? Further, who do you need to jettison from your network because they are having a negative impact on your ability to function at your peak in your HR practice? Finally, we're *Hustling* – actually doing something about our network and building bridges with the people who matter.

Sort through your current network – Do you already have a network, and what sort of network is it? Who's in there that you perhaps haven't served as well as you could have? Who could add to your future success?

Search for your *Core Four* – Who are the four key individuals you must have in your network? Why are they so critical? If they're not in your network already, why not? What do you know about them (or need to know) that can assist you get 'in' with them in order for you to serve them better?

Seek out those people who have a broad and significantly influential network already – who has a network that you can you leverage? Who is important in the area that you want to develop in? How will you make contact with them?

Sink those in your network who shouldn't be there – Are there people you're associated with who have a negative or toxic brand? Is the balance between giving and taking horribly uneven in a particular relationship? Is someone dragging down your ability to fulfil your potential as a Catalyst? Who do you need to break ties with?

This last strategy is difficult, because it requires judgement and drawing a line on your past and present. It forces you to actively triage your relationships. This trait often singles out Catalysts from the average HR practitioner. The choice doesn't need to be disrespectful, damaging or undignified, but the choice is yours to make. Choose wisely.

Some additional questions that may help you select who you need to connect better with include:

Who do you need to trust better, more, deeper? Why them?

How easy are you to connect with – how accessible are you in person and online at work?

What gets in the way of people trying to contact you?

What do you put in the way that (a) you're aware of, and (b) you're not currently aware of?

Who's on your radar and who might you have missed? Why are they important?

Who matters in your future success as an HR Catalyst? Why?

Maintaining Relationships

Now that you are aware of *who* you need to deepen your connection with at work, we need to turn our attention to *how* Catalyst HR practitioners can most effectively do so. We'll start by diving deep into what makes those relationships click. Think about the actual relationship – the connection you have with each individual:

What is it that you enjoy about the people closest to you?

What are the themes or patterns across that group?

What are the situations and context in which you interact?

How do these contribute towards a a positive and fruitful relationship?

This type of analysis will help you develop a strategy for connecting and building relationships with those you've already assessed as important to your future HR success.

You now need to be in the places where those people are. There is little point being known by and knowing key people, if you're not with them to make better use of that connection. Yes, you can leverage technology, but nothing beats the human connection of being present, in-person with others. A great place to start is the support and administration staff across your organisation. Often taken for granted, these people are the nodes that connect the business like a network – they have access to senior leaders (and their calendars) and are a great resource to call upon when you face time with those people of influence across the business. Get 'in' with these people and you have an 'in' with any of the influencers.

It always pays to be connected to those who have little positional authority but relatively large levels of practical power. So, look across your organisation, perhaps with a structure chart, and conduct an audit of who you're connected with and where. Where are the gaps? Who are those people and who do you know who could help you connect with them? Conversely, what are the areas you're heavily connected with – which relationships can you leverage here into other areas of the business? Who knows who and how strong are their connections? Importantly, what do you need to learn about those people you are now going to attempt to collaborate with?

Elsewhere in the organisation, other good resources are new or front-line managers known as having high potential. Senior leaders like to be associated with high-potentials and to claim mentoring roles in their success. If you're respected and liked by these people, they can help your brand with those further up the food chain, while also helping them to achieve more. It goes both ways – these are opportunities for win-win relationships that you both can leverage. Being in HR, you'll be aware of who the up-and-coming future leaders and star performers are. How can you help them reach their potential sooner? This starts by getting to know them and being of service to them – even if they aren't in positions of authority yet. Remember – HR is there to serve. But be careful not to undermine the managers of these high-potentials. Keep them in the loop. You're not trying to steal their relationship, you're trying to foster your own one with both parties.

You then need to build, maintain and nurture each and every relationship. This requires focus and an approach based on operating in-service of each person. Treat everyone like a customer and go above their expectations. It pays to keep an inventory of the relationships you have, so that you can regularly audit how each is progressing. Like any customer-facing role, you need to put in the work. If you think about a great customer experience you've had recently, say at a shop or retail outlet - what was it that made it so good? More than likely it was the personal connection and/or the manner in what the person serving you went above your expectations – conscious or unconscious. These moments spark a shift in people's perceptions – you should be thinking of ways to spark a similar shift in the hearts and minds of those you serve as an HR Catalyst. Who requires some attention right now, why, and what does the best version of that attention look like for them?

Essentially, you need to treat all key individuals as a separate market as if you were a sales person targeting them, except that you don't push a product or any type of sales. The process is the same simply in that that the lead-up is about learning all you can. How do you learn all you can about new individuals in your network? You already read about a fantastic approach to doing this in chapters 1-3! Now's the time to apply it to each key individual:

What **insight** do you need to have about them?

What are their strategies, issues, concerns, operating context, history, worries and fears?

What are their strengths and weaknesses, their aspirations and motivations?

How can you help them be **unattached**?

What might they need your help surrendering or letting-go of?

> How might you go about that as a colleague?
>
> What do you need to **focus** on that could build a better relationship?
>
> What are the things you have heard about them from others – are they true or false?
>
> How will you use these insights?

Have Better Conversations

Most often, better relationships start with a conversation. Catalyst HR practitioners are highly skilled in the art of conversation (although be careful not to interpret this as having the 'gift of the gab', as this may see you viewed more as a used car salesperson, and not a deep listener with empathy for their concerns). *The Art of Conversation* is in fact the title of Catherine Blyth's "guided tour of a neglected pleasure" where she defines conversation as requiring two or more people, and both *interest* and *attention*. Without interest and attention we have ourselves at best, a lecture, and at worst, a severe power imbalance. These are not the conversations of a Catalyst.

Meaningful dialogue is the aim of every conversation you want to be having – a conversation that adds value to the person you're speaking with and adds value to your credibility. Critical in every conversation you have is the stance that you are there to serve, but not to simply do things for your customer. Serving may be advising them to rethink their strategy or to not go down a path you believe will have negative consequences. It may mean probing them a bit more with an uncomfortable line of questioning that sees them build clarity and conviction, or it may see them realise they got something wrong or don't yet have all the context required to make a robust decision.

Showing interest and paying attention are actions – things that can be observed. They not only show engagement, but grow engagement, between those included in the conversation.

"To show engagement is to grow engagement"

A key component of having better conversations is not necessarily the quality of what is spoken, but the quality of the listening that takes place. Oscar Trimboli, author of *Deep Listening,* uses what he calls the 125 to 400 rule to explain why we find this so difficult. It's an interesting fact that we speak an average of 125 words per minute, but can hear up to 400 words in the same amount of time. So, when people speak to us there is a 'gap' that we tend to fill in with our own noise – self-talk, chatter, observations, and what we want to say. We tend to hear keywords and prepare to respond, which stops us listening to the rest of what the other person is saying. We get ready to launch into our spiel, despite the fact that it's more than likely already off topic by the time we speak! To make matters worse, the speaker can think at about 900 words per minute. This means they're already feeling like they can't communicate everything they want to, even before we jump in to the first gap with our own opinion.

Given HR is about people, it's imperative we develop our ability to listen to what is really being said. This is about the essence, the underlying messages, and what isn't being spoken out loud. Interestingly, researchers have concluded that we

(a) drop out of conversations every twelve to eighteen seconds to process what people are saying; and (b) often remember what we think about what another person is saying, because that is a stronger internal process and chemical signal. In other words, our internal listening and dialogue trumps the other person's speech. So, next time you speak with a colleague, take a quick audit of your thought processes – are you triaging their words... or your own?

You see, the whole point of having better conversation is to build on the connection you have and use conversation to take the relationship to a new level. Then, and only then, can you spark the change required in other people. Connection. Relationship. Impact (preferably in that sequence). Each conversation should have a purpose and an outcome for both parties. Try not to be too formulaic with this, but it's important you have a reason for the chat. After all, you're both busy, so the conversations you have need to add more value than would be gained undertaking a different task on your 'to-do' list. A next-level conversation may even be to ask your customers in a way that is sincere, polite and most importantly you, "What is important for you in this conversation and what does a great outcome look, feel and sound like to you?" This demonstrates to them that you respect their time and want to make the conversation as productive as possible for them. Over time you won't need to ask these questions – as the relationship is bolstered, you will both have a clear way of having better conversations. They'll become more efficient and effective for you both. In the beginning though, it is vital you tread carefully and not get labelled as always having an agenda. Use your self-awareness to pick your moments – perhaps the agenda is simply to grow the personal connection and enjoy moments of friendship at work. These are important building blocks of better, more productive relationships.

Judith Glaser, author of *Conversational Intelligence,* believes conversations change the landscape, while Theodore Zeldin, author and philosopher of all-things conversation once said "conversation doesn't just reshuffle the cards, it creates new cards" – again, to show engagement is to grow engagement. In both cases, we are gaining something new to work with. These wonderful concepts outline the limitless potential inherent in having better conversations about work, at work. We all have a brand and want to be known for something. Sometimes our wants and needs are the same thing; other times they conflict. Seeking alignment between *wants* and *haves* with regard to how others perceive us around the workplace is key. In fact, being known for your ability to speak with impact to a diverse range of key influencers across your organisation positions you for a bright future as an HR Catalyst. It just takes some attention and purposeful practice.

Matt Church, founder of Thought Leaders Global, advises we take a "Yes, and .." approach to our conversations. Most HR practitioners are known for taking a more risk-averse and patch-protective stance in a conversation, or "Yes, but ..." response. This latter stance tends to put the brakes on conversations and relationships, resulting in the HR practitioner being labelled as negative or the fun-police. HR's effectiveness can be measured by the state of the relationships it holds; those relationships can be measured by the quality of the conversations had within those relationships. Taking a "yes, and ...." approach in your conversations demonstrates you understand what they are trying to say or do, and that you want to help enable that to happen by adding to the goodness they've thought about with your own take on things. This is a true partnership at work – where the sum is greater than the separate parts.

Fundamentally, HR is about conversations. We espouse best-practice leadership, performance management and team development processes, without realising they are all based on managers and staff right across every organisation talking about the stuff that matters. The 'Leader as Coach' philosophy is all about facilitating better conversations with and between staff. All performance management and development processes are underpinned by an ability to connect staff and leaders through frequent and relevant conversations. It is thus imperative that HR as a function leads by example, and the HR Catalyst has an opportunity to lead the way for the profession. People are often watching and waiting for HR to make the first move – we can no longer issue edicts and policy only to be seen to not behave as we expect the rest of the organisation to do so. It's time we moved HR from the threat of being branded "Do as we say; not as we do" to "Do as we do". Through developing our conversational abilities, HR can be the team, the function and the leaders that all other teams and leaders want to be like.

Another way to develop better relationships with colleagues and customers is through storytelling. Framing your point from the perspective of an example – with your own or a third party – helps customers imagine for themselves the scenario you're trying to paint. They invest a little bit of themselves in the story, which allows for a great conversation as questions are asked or points are raised where the interest is piqued. Stories also have the potential to bring humour to a situation. There's a reason stories are funny. It's like the difference between swearing if you're quoting someone, and actually swearing. Stories give you a licence to be more extreme, or ridiculous, or engaging, while still making an important point to your audience.

So how do we know how to tell a good story? Gabrielle Dolan, elite speaker and author of many books on the art of storytelling, says quite simply that a story has a start, a middle and an end. Often, we omit one of these segments and the story falls flat. For example, we can get caught up in the set-up, building up expectation only to rush the ending. She also points out that stories need to match the context and purpose for the conversation. Relevance is in the ear of the listener. There is little point using examples from the accounting industry when talking to people on the meat-processing line! You're better to have learned their context early and researched stories that fit their context. Better still, ask them for some stories, so that they become the experts and teach you. It's imperative HR Catalysts choose their stories wisely and ensure any examples are in the language of the listener.

When thinking about the stories you want to weave into the conversations you have with your customers, make sure they are not too self-indulgent. Personal stories are certainly a great way to build rapport and show vulnerability (a key trait of the HR Catalyst as we'll see in chapter 5) but over-doing the self-disclosure can minimise the focus on the customer's situation and undo any empathy you have displayed. Bottom line – stay on point and be attention-out with a focus on what serves them. Above all, you must be yourself in each and everything you do – your work, your ways of connecting, and what it is you get known for.

Key questions to consider before we move on to the final dimension of the Catalyst model include:

Ever wondered or even noticed what you actually do while someone is talking to you?

Observe and reflect on what's going on in your mind as they speak. What are you noticing?

What is your mind's voice saying?

What signals are you giving-off with your gestures, facial expressions, posture?

How actively interested are you and are you paying attention?

Would the person you're conversing with be able to tell?

Seek out some feedback on how well you listen, show interest and pay attention — why do people say what they say about you?

What sort of conversations do you need to have? Why? How will you start these?

How would you rate your conversational intelligence?

How could you use storytelling to have / enable better conversations about work at work?

Which conversations have you been putting off? Which one will you start today?

CHAPTER FIVE

Yourself

BE	DO	HAVE
Insightful	Understand	Greater Empathy
Unattached	Surrender	Deeper Wisdom
Focused	Hustle	Meaningful Progress
Connected	Collaborate	Stronger Connection
Yourself	Believe	True Presence

Yourself

> *"Be yourself; everyone else is taken."*
>
> – Oscar Wilde

If you have ever been around someone who's completely comfortable in their own skin, you will have felt the power of authenticity. The simple art of being true to yourself – to truly live – is the final dimension of the Catalyst model of HR practice. It's about belief in who you are, and how you can genuinely impact the world around yourself. It's one of the deepest beliefs you can hold, and it leads to true presence. Believing in yourself is a lever that opens up opportunities; without it people see through what you say and do. What's worse is that without belief, you see through yourself – and that shows. The most amazing people-solution can be undone by an HR practitioner who lacks belief in themselves and / or their solution. Believing in the work you do begins with believing in yourself.

Yet, referring to this dimension as something to 'practice' somewhat diminishes the value of authentically being yourself. There's a risk that we try so hard to be the person we think others want or need us to be, that we turn ourselves into something we're not. The purpose of this dimension is not to add so many layers to our personality that we mask who we are. Instead, it's about being true to your word, your purpose and your principles. For something that's a simple 'way of being', we make it incredibly awkward and difficult at times! Indeed, being real does take a whole lot of practice. HR Catalysts must know what it means to be true to themselves and work on that truth.

This final dimension is placed here because it's imperative we are reminded to be ourselves in how we go about gaining *insightful* context, our customers wants and need, the game of HR and our brand of practicing our profession. Likewise, we must be genuinely *unattached* to all that is holding us back from better, more authentic practice. The *focus* we apply in our practice via the projects and initiatives we put in place must be real and meaningful, and the momentum must be self-driven for it to stick. Finally, the *connection* you nurture and grow in pursuit of a better experience as a people professional needs to feel right, to be values-based and free of competitive agenda. This is the act of being in-service, and an HR Catalyst's service must come from within themselves. In essence, being ourselves brings us full-circle around the Catalyst model to land us back at being insightful. How well do we really know ourselves and how does this bolster our ability to practice HR authentically?

However, it's unfortunate that HR professionals are sometimes known for being less than genuine. I have witnessed many a well-meaning HR practitioner talk about an initiative designed to lift an individual or team out of a rut, knowing too well they expect it to fail. I recall a time quite early in my own career working with a particular manager who was tired of (from their perspective) having to put up with the poor performance of a couple of his staff. In discussing options with my HR manager, we agreed with my customer's proposal to restructure the under-performers out of the team. This is in direct contrast to a catalyst approach. At the time this seemed like a rite-or-passage (at least I was told as such), but I soon realised this was not the practice of someone who is authentic and true to their values. Just because a leader is frustrated does not give them licence to give up leading. It's HR's role to enable both this leader and their staff to find ways to be the best versions of themselves every day. In this instance, all I enabled was for a lazy manager to get away with not doing their own job. Taking a stand for what is right and for what you believe in can be difficult – especially for those early in their careers – but it's a necessary part of the role.

In general, the HR profession is flush with people who hold themselves to very high standards. While we can all think of isolated cases where HR may have let itself down, it seems other functions across business have an undue negative view of the Human Resources profession. Not only is this unfortunate, it's also largely untrue.

So where does this perception come from? I suspect its inherent in the very nature of the work HR performs – the fine line we tread between open, honest communication and the need to keep elements of employee experiences of work (both positive and negative) private. It's difficult to balance workplace tensions. For example, in many interactions people are looking to be confirmed as 'right', when in actual fact it's about finding a solution for both parties to reach a happy medium. On the other hand, sometimes people and their behaviour are simply wrong and don't fit what the organisation is trying to achieve, yet they can't or won't see the bigger picture. Additionally, you just need to trawl the internet reading articles on why HR isn't trusted to see examples of where people have been burned from privacy and confidentiality breaches by errant HR professionals. But these are the minority. By far the majority of people in HR are good, honest, values-driven individuals and like in most situations, it only takes a small few to tarnish a whole lot. Sometimes it takes a thick skin to work in HR.

Many HR professionals also suffer from serial Impostor Syndrome. This is a statement I will no doubt cop a lot of flak for, but I stand by it. I'm not saying HR people are impostors, far from it. I'm saying we believe it. HR professionals often feel out of their depth, as if sooner or later people will find out we are not as capable as others believe. The HR profession does require the occasional instance of 'fake-it-til-you-make-it', as sometimes we need to put on a brave face and deal with the matter at hand. Other times we're going to show that we feel out of our depths. I believe this is not only ok, but the opportunity for HR Catalysts to own these feelings.

Showing vulnerability is not only an act of authenticity, but it also builds rapport with others. You'd be surprised how often breaking down walls with honesty leads the way for others to open up, by speaking to the vibe in the room. Seeking clarification in a meeting with high-powered executives on important points you don't understand positions you in far greater light than trying to 'save-face', keep quiet and hide your panic. People appreciate others seeking to understand – it displays interest and attention, while letting others into your world view. Be yourself, always. Don't ever compromise on this. The people who matter most will value you for it in the long run.

In this chapter we'll cover the HR Catalyst's need to practice:

1. Being genuine;
2. Showing empathy;
3. Being present
4. Fostering trust

Being genuine

Socrates is said to have expanded on the Greek maxim "Know thyself" by stating the "unexamined life is not worth living". Have you examined your life? The first element of being yourself is to be genuine, and to be genuine you need to know who you are. So, who are you? What does the real, genuine you look like? Take out a piece of paper and write ten words that describe you from your own perspective. Next, write ten words that people at work would use to describe you. Read both lists – chances are there will be some difference across the two. Which list is your wish-list, and which is closer to fact?

Often it is difficult to put into words who we really are. Self-awareness is a tricky truth to mine – no matter how deep you dig, there's always more to learn about yourself. Along the way you'll hit rocks of self-doubt and cave-ins of denial. When asked to describe our true selves, we stumble, stutter, and feel put on the spot. When we finally think we've got the words, as we speak them, we get distracted by the chatter in our heads saying "Nah, no that's not it." Don't second guess your own beliefs. This is so unhelpful and it diminishes the value we have to offer. It is critical we get to the bottom of who we are, and a big part of this is learning to have faith in your perception of self.

So, what is a genuine HR Catalyst? Is it how you come across to others; how they receive you? Or, is your genuineness restricted to the belief and feeling you have within yourself – even if you may never be able to convey this to others? In other words, is it about you or them? The inner you or the outer you? To answer this, let's go back to the need for some context.

The premise of this book is based on a model of better HR practice that sets-up go-getting people professionals for a better future. It's a framework and approach to practicing HR that is not only more fulfilling for the professional, but one that sees real change initiated in others for greater individual, team and organisational success. This approach connects the practitioner with the work required to provide world-class service to their customers across the organisation. HR Catalysts achieve success through *how* they practice, more so than what they do day-to-day. HR Catalysts are doers. They're known for 'doing' HR in a fresh way that, at its foundation, has a focus on being of service to each and every customer and their teams. They serve the organisation by ensuring everything they do is an action that advances the organisation closer to its desired and planned success. HR Catalysts are purposeful, as well as flexible. In all their tasks they are conscious of how they are perceived by others – in the working world of the HR Catalyst, actions certainly speak louder than words. How you behave is what people notice, so your behaviour must appear genuine to your customers.

So, how do you know how you're perceived by others around you? Simple. Ask them! We have highlighted the need for the HR Catalyst to be in touch with customers and to understand their brand of HR practice by asking how you're received; how easy you are to work with and what you are known for. Now it's time to go deeper – perhaps by following up with those who gave you the original feedback and ask:

What about you is different from others in HR they have worked with?

What are three characteristics that describe you and how you work with that person?

What, if anything, is unique about the way you work?

What about you do they believe is 100% genuine?

How others perceive us – especially what they let on about – helps to build our self-identity, yet we're not simply at the mercy of other's views. How we are perceived is only part of the picture. It's also important to reflect on how you 'feel' about yourself, because this drives how much you invest of yourself into your practice, your work, and your interactions with colleagues and customers. Your own self-view can enable or equally disable your performance and effectiveness by driving how you show-up at work. You'll have seen this right throughout your career – the person with a negative self-image that tries to mask this by either (intentionally or sub-consciously) over-doing or under-cooking emotions, vulnerability or sharing. This isn't great from anybody across the organisation, but it's close to unforgivable in HR. You see, HR should be the exemplar of not only team and leadership behaviours, but what it means to be an employee in your workplace. Yes, you can be human and have bad days, but the HR Catalyst knows themselves well enough to pick up on the signals, the early-warning system that alerts you to a need to take timeout or to change your perspective or approach. Self-awareness goes a long way in the practice of HR, and the organisation takes a long time to forget the day a member of the HR team has a shocker!

At this point it is useful to reflect on what it feels like to be you in the people profession. Ask yourself these questions:

What do I believe about the HR profession?

Where do I see myself fitting in that belief?

What do I know to be true about myself?

What do I want others to believe about me?

Why are they important to me? Am I those things now? How big is the gap?

Am I enough?

How proud do your answers make you feel? Ponder this. That last one is a beauty. If the answer is not an immediate "Yes", do yourself a favour: STOP looking to be more! You're most likely reading this book because you have an unsettling feeling that you have more potential to offer and that the people profession has more to give, perhaps differently from how it gives now. Often, we struggle to define what enough looks like. We wrestle with our thoughts and feelings trying to quantify it, but maybe the point isn't volume… it's quality. Rather than thinking about numbers, think of feelings. How it feels to be you as an HR practice is more valuable than the number of times you interacted with a customer while trying to be that way.

Maybe you're not sure how to fulfil your potential. My hope and intention is that this book helps you uncover, unlock and in some way, unleash that potential. Striving to be an HR Catalyst should not be a mission to validate yourself – your purpose and reason for being on this planet. You are in fact already enough; it's time the world saw the awesome you that already exists. And it's time for you to accept yourself. Let's get back to work.

Showing empathy

While technology is streamlining work and freeing-teams-up for deeper thinking and more collaborative work, people remain the future of work. It makes sense then, that individuals and whole workforces need to connect and relate to a diverse range of people as we move from project to project, team to team. Being the people profession and having the term 'human' in our title means it's imperative we show the way.

As a focused operator who keeps in touch with current thinking about all things HR, you'll know how showing empathy is being touted as the critical skill, behaviour and ability needed in the workplaces of the future. I believe this to be true, and nowhere is this more paramount than in the people profession. You may have just responded to that last sentence with "Yes, of course. That's stating the obvious!" Yet, empathy as a concept is bandied about as if everyone understands what is meant by the term. HR must exemplify empathy in everything we do – the work that inspires and drives greater performance, and the work that results in other people lives to be altered towards the negative.

Empathy, however, is largely misunderstood and mistaken for sympathy. Empathy is your ability to recognise the feelings and emotional state of others and understand what they are experiencing. It's often referred to as being able to walk in someone else's shoes. It's also almost always associated with emotions we recognise as negative – sadness, anger, being upset. Using a definition like this in the workplace has detrimental effects, as it skews initiatives and conversations to those negative things. It predominantly speaks to those aspects of life in the workplace we think we should minimise, hence the large focus on wellness and wellbeing (which is appropriate as society tackles integrating working into life and vice-versa).

In my view, this is only half the story and leaves out large swathes of opportunity. Empathy is also about being able to recognise and understand what lights people up, what they define as success and why they choose to celebrate something. It might be something that you might not celebrate to the same extent, but you respect their right to do so and in fact applaud and celebrate with and for them. For example, you may be working with a sales team that has collectively struggled to hit their targets. Under the guidance of their manager, they reviewed their targets and broke them down into manageable sub-targets that take into account workload and working hours spread across the team. Having made small gains in achieving these new targets, they choose to celebrate these wins – wins that in your work may be every-day, but you recognise and respect that what matters is what's meaningful to the team. This is the empathy HR Catalysts should help foster in the workplace. Be careful, however, not to over-do it. It's a balancing act between joining others to celebrate the many small but meaningful wins, while also motivating people to strive and push for more.

Consider:

Are you an emotionally intelligent HR practitioner? How do you know?

Reflect on a time when someone at work showed an emotion you couldn't relate to – what was happening in that instance?

How do you react when you see other people celebrating success?

What role could your HR team play in fostering greater empathy in your workplace?

What could you in your role show greater empathy towards?

Being present

The third element of being yourself is your ability to be present in the moment, with others. You should be there with people and not give in to distractions when others require your undivided attention (i.e. pretty much anytime you interact with a customer). Such an ability is the essence of customer-centricity.

Have you ever been into a shop and had the retail assistant deal with you in a way that made you feel like they have been waiting all day just for you to arrive? Catalysts bring this sense of dedication and devotion to customers within their organisations. It's almost a sixth sense – the ability to tune in to a person's wavelength and meet them there. The best at this are masters in quickly finding common ground with those they are working with – again, a savvy line of questioning that feels more like a conversation is the best place to start. Be outwardly-facing in your ability to be fully present.

The flip-side of this example is when you aren't even acknowledged by anyone in the shop. As your frustration grows with people not doing their job, you start to fester and exaggerate. Making matters worse is that (hopefully rare) instance when the shop assistant makes you feel you're disturbing them or in the way (as opposed to the person potentially paying their wages!). I'm not suggesting you have to be all to everyone – especially in a crowded meeting. What I am stating, quite categorically, is that you need to bring your A-game to work. This means looking for and making the most of every opportunity to create moments with people individually.

It may be as simple as a small acknowledgement with a nod of the head to someone across the room to let them know you noticed them. It may be a referring to a colleague in a meeting as possibly having a view on this matter, and would they like to share it? Even better, you might get up from your desk and personally visit someone as they work. The HR professional would say they were "Just passing by so thought I'd pop in and say 'hi'"; the HR Catalyst would say "I've been thinking about that point you made last time we spoke and wonder how you're feeling? I could have called, but it the subject seemed important to you. Not expecting we discuss it now, as it might not suit, but when it does, let me know. I've got some ideas."

Turning more inward, let's think about how you stay present in the moment. Is your mind always racing with ideas and/or busyness? Do you have control over who you are being?

Being present is a concept that places importance on both words, not just the latter. How you are being is critical to your ability to stay present in the situation you are in. Being is not doing – it comes from your subconscious which means it happens automatically. The way to influence this is to create different habits. Again, being yourself takes practice!

How do we build the skill of being present? It's easy to acknowledge that it's important in both concept and practice, that we want to do it, that we recognise how it will improve our impact with customers. But how do we actually go about being more present, when we currently possess a whole lot of habits that work directly against it?

The practice of mindfulness is gaining traction within workplaces across the globe. Mindfulness is the ability to achieve a mental state that focuses your awareness on the present moment, while calmly acknowledging and accepting your feelings, thoughts, and sensations. It's about moving from a full mind to a mind fully aware of the present. This can be achieved at work through the surrendering process and speaks to the heart of what it means to be fully present. In a practical sense it's about where you spend your focus and energy - what is a priority and what can wait?

At a deeper level and with a customer, a mindfulness practice can help you tune into their frequency. Remember Oscar Trimboli's 125 to 400 rule? The HR Catalyst needs to work out how to calm the noise and internal chatter than comes with being keen and excited. Curb your enthusiasm, and instead listen and observe. Tune in to who they are being – do their words match their body language? Use the silence; don't feel compelled to fill it in. This is thinking space for you both. Most of all, breathe. This sounds a bit woo-woo, but if you are the type of person who finds themselves looking for constant action and progress, perhaps you could benefit from pausing and taking a moment to enjoy the time with others. You may find this opens up space for better conversations as people (and you) relax.

An active way to practice mindfulness and meditation is through yoga. Western commercialism has turned the lay-person's understanding of what yoga is to be all about needing to be flexible enough to fold yourself into weird and wonderful postures. In fact, these poses or asana are a small percentage of what a full yoga practice entails, and were only developed as a means to facilitate more conscious focus on the breath. If you've ever practiced yoga you'll have noticed how movements that extend, open or broaden the body are executed with an inhalation, while movements that close, twist or make the physical shape smaller require an exhalation. Yet, even this language is misleading, because the movements are designed to facilitate each breath; not the other way around. In essence, yoga is breath. While you might be mocked for popping into a yoga pose mid-meeting, the HR Catalyst would be well served tuning in to the breath when you find yourself overwhelmed or unable to focus. Being in control of you enables you to control situations and influence others. Consider:

How available are you to your customers/client?

In what way could you be more available while also protecting your time?

When you hear consistent feedback about yourself, what do you think? Do you accept it?

What does someone being present with you look like, sound and feel like?

Do you also display these traits with others? Have you asked anybody lately?

What drains your attention at work?

How might you change the situation?

Fostering trust

Fostering trust is ultimately how you, the HR Catalyst, will spark change in others and amplify your impact within your organisation. The greater the trust others have in you; the greater your ability is to influence them towards higher, better, and more productivity (and ultimately a greater experience of work). You'll be well aware from your own practice that a lack of trust between people, teams and across organisations can be the death-nail for progress and performance. The most well-intentioned strategy can easily be undone by a lack of trust between individuals. Similarly, for the HR Catalyst, trust is paramount for getting traction with customers. When you are trusted, people will give you a chance over those they don't trust. Likewise, when you're not trusted, you will have a hard job trying to convince people of even the most clear-cut and obvious path to take.

Trust has multiple levels – you could think of it as the layers of earth beneath your feet. At the surface level is the grass growing in relatively porous top-soil. It's the layer where any manner of material can seep into. Think of this as light, expectant trust – the trust you have that someone will turn up to a meeting at the scheduled time. Next is the sub-soil and clay, a denser less porous layer that still allows water and dissolved minerals to seep. This layer of trust is harder to get to but not impossible with some effort. It's also a relatively thin layer itself. The third layer is rock, which is deep down, consistent and solid – formed over a longer period of time. This represents trust that has been uncovered through dedicated effort, but once tapped into is very robust and hard to move from its foundation. Like digging a post hole for house foundations, you need to dig into the firmer layer deep down, which if building trust, take time and effort.

Whether you believe trust is something first given to be taken away, or that trust should first be earned, isn't up for debate. There's a whole lot of complicated belief systems about trust, but they're not the point here. What I do know is that deep trust takes time to truly build, but is quickly eroded. I also know that over the time it takes to foster a trusting relationship in the workplace, multiple interactions need to take place and that within each interaction there needs to be a moment that your customer stops and says to themselves "Wow – I wasn't expecting that!" These are the moments when you both click, tuning in to one-another, and the customer realises you get their world. Priceless! So, how intentional are you with picking your moments?

It's no mistake the most effective team development models all include an element of trust as a foundation. And how is this foundation built? Through vulnerability. Often now referred to as 'psychological safety', this trust is built around an individual's (a) ability and (b) willingness to demonstrate vulnerability to others. Being vulnerable allows others to let down their guard and open up to better conversations, new ideas and ultimately change their worldview. It's a license to thrive together. Not many HR professionals fully grasp the implications of this – they understand that leaders should demonstrate vulnerability, but they themselves operate at arms-length from their own team, their customers, and even the rest of the organisation. If this is you, again, STOP. Get known by others for who you are and what you represent.

This isn't about introverts and extroverts either. Vulnerability is a skill all HR Catalysts, regardless of personality traits, preferences or persuasion, must display. It might be uncomfortable at first, but the pay-off can be immense. It's also not about being weak in front of others. Vulnerability is a strength; incompetence is a weakness. In fact, if anything there are people waiting for leaders to show vulnerability – we've agreed HR is a leadership role, so it's time HR really put the human into the profession and showed some vulnerability. This starts with you – the individual practitioner.

Your credibility as an HR Catalyst also rests on the actions you take in your work. Remember, this framework sits on the foundation of understanding your customer groups' context and surrendering what might hold you back from learning more about that context. What better way to do this than to go to your customers and offer to pitch in with something they're working on? Maybe they'll give you dud tasks or throw you in the deep-end. Jump at the opportunity to learn more about their world by getting your hands dirty. It'll do wonders for your HR brand. Showing that you're not afraid to (a) pitch in, and (b) recognise you're not as good at a task as they are as the experts, builds greater rapport than any words you speak. In this context, actions most certainly speak louder than words.

Being yourself, believing in that person and demonstrating true presence in each moment is ultimately about values – what are yours and do they align with the people you work with? They may not be exactly the same, but your values should enable you to operate effectively and professionally with others, even with those with whom you don't see eye-to-eye or even warm to. How you deal with these people and foster strong working relationship in the face of an apparent values mismatch can be a critical test in your ability to operate as a high-functioning HR practitioner.

Ultimately, you'll recognise the need to maintain professionalism at all times. This means following-through on your commitments, maintaining appropriate confidentiality, building sufficient trust in the minds of those you serve (regardless of whether you necessarily trust them to the same standard) and persevering in your quest to assist the organisation reach its strategic goals.

With all this in mind, consider:

Do you demonstrate vulnerability in your HR practice? How so?

In what way to ensure your customers trust you? How do you know that works for them?

Is the brand and reputation of your HR function appropriate, relevant and useful?

Seek feedback from a customer you took some time to 'click' with and ask when the moment was they turned a page with you? What happened in them?

What did you do to facilitate that? How could you replicate this with other customers?

Look at your behaviour within your own team – do you act differently with some colleagues than others? How so? Why?

Find a team you need to foster greater trust with and offer to help them with something they're working on.

CHAPTER SIX

Unleashing
the Catalyst

Unleashing the Catalyst

"The best time to plant a tree is 20 years ago. The second-best time is now."

— Chinese Proverb

Throughout this book we have canvassed many ways and means for you to uncover your potential to do and be more in your HR career by taking a trip around the Catalyst model of HR practice. Knowing you have that potential is what made you pick up this book and start reading it. You had the desire to inspire and influence people across your organisation on a deeper, more profound and impactful level – you simply needed a method of unlocking that potential.

In chapter 1 we looked into the need for you, the HR Catalyst, to be *insightful* by understanding the context in which you and your customers operate. In doing so, you deliver an HR service with greater empathy, taking into account the character and nature of the people you serve. Next, we looked at how you can offer deeper wisdom to the managers and teams you work with by *surrendering* the things in your past that hold you back and prevent you from uncovering and unlocking potential – both yours and those you serve. In essence, chapter 2 examined ways to become *unattached* to the past and pre-conceptions of how work could and should be done, and asked questions to help you to help your customers let-go of what may be holding them back as well.

Chapter 3 then looked into the need for you to be more *focused* in your HR practice – to make more meaningful progress through the act of prioritising work and going deep on fewer tasks in order to gain more traction. In essence this chapter was about practicing with more hustle. It was only then in chapter 4 that we began to explore the need for the HR Catalyst to have stronger connections with people across the organisation and to leverage these better through collaboration. Indeed, the *connected* HR Catalyst becomes a leader of far more than HR when they build a network of savvy operators around them to get better work done.

Finally, in chapter 5 we examined the crucial need for you, the insightful, unattached, focused and connected HR Catalyst, to be *yourself*. You are already enough and have the nous, technical skill and knowledge to build the experiences you now require to take your HR service to the next level. You simply need to believe in yourself. When you believe in what you do, how you do it and the importance of doing it your way; when you believe in who you are and the uniqueness you bring to your HR practice, only then will you have the true presence that sees those key people in your business gravitate to you for your expertise. This is how you flip the model of you working harder to get their attention. Ultimately, the HR Catalyst becomes the go-to person in the organisation for sound strategic partnerships.

The ultimate quest

Moving from *doing* to *being* is ultimately the quest of the HR Catalyst – to *do less* in order to *be more* for the people you serve. While your manner of practice is all about serving your customer managers, from a selfish perspective, *being* also results in a far more rewarding experience of work for you – the reader of this book and the future of the people profession.

But why stop there? What if there was more?

Traditionally, HR careers start in a transactional mode of working. You learn the ropes by providing advice and assistance on an as-needed basis, usually to frontline managers. In these HR roles there is a lot of doing – responding, informing, advising and implementing – activity that sees tasks get done towards a bigger plan or set of objectives. Task lists and checkboxes dominate the day-to-day work undertaken at this level. It's where repetition helps to reinforce learning. It's also a time when any mistakes you make are not career threatening, nor is the fall-out from those mistakes too great for your customers. You can usually recover your brand and credibility quickly.

Over time, working with managers and leaders sees the HR professional develop a degree of rapport and comfort around their customers – both the people and the work they undertake. They aclimatise and understand aspects of how that business functions. The risk here is that they become too comfortable and are thus blocked from exploring new ideas or challenging the status quo. It is at this point that work starts to move from transactional to transformational – where the reactive to-and-fro between HR and customers turns into more proactive partnering with a wider group of leaders across the business. It's also a stage where your mistakes can have lasting impact on your career and the business. As you operate at a higher level, with greater responsibility comes greater risk. In particular, being insightful and focused here starts to pay dividends.

Here, HR is required to operate with greater insight. Practitioners are expected to use their intuition in reading not only what is happening, but also what might happen in the future. Should a particular course of action be taken, they must be able to develop options and initiatives to suit. This tipping point is also one that sees HR practitioners make a choice – to remain in the transactional space delivering subject matter expertise and developing a brand of technical mastery, or to relinquish some day-to-day tasks in order to operate at a more strategic level. The step up here is to move to coaching leaders, a role that requires savvy influencing skills. Leveraging these skills further sees you delivering greater impact on the business, sector, industry and potentially the greater HR profession.

Nowadays, with the explosive growth and uptake of Big Data, Artificial Intelligence and people metrics, HR professionals are expected to interpret patterns and develop insights a lot earlier in their careers than they were 10-15 years ago. This in itself exaccerbates the need to operate in a catalyst-like manner.

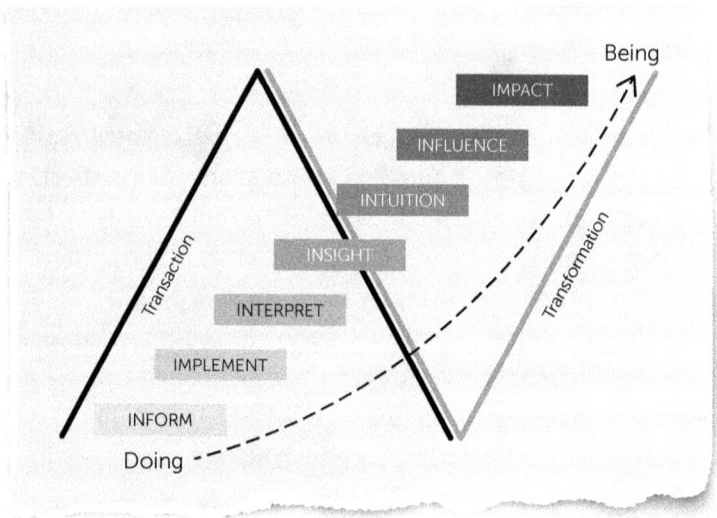

Regardless of how long you have been in HR, you're probably looking back on your career and thinking "I wish I had taken this approach years ago!" But remind yourself of the Chinese proverb at the start of this chapter – planting a tree is just like investing in real estate or saving money. The best time to develop what's needed today was in the past – most likely many years ago. But you now have in front of you the opportunity to perform some amazing work in the future, starting right now. So rather than dwell on what you might have been and done, start now. *Be* the catalyst that sparks change in those you serve. Surrender thoughts and feelings of what might have been, if only ….. and seek greater insight into exactly what you need to do from here.

Ultimately, this book is about unleashing the best version of you. It's about moving from *doing* stuff *to* and *for* the managers you serve as customers, to *being* what they need *with* them. It's about *how* they will best be served to see them excel in their roles. By unleashing your Catalyst HR practice upon your organisation, you will spark purposeful, lasting change in people, teams and divisions. You'll see them achieve performance and outcomes that would have been impossible without your dedicated approach to serving them and their achievement of the business' vision and mission.

So, now you know *how* to be the next HR Catalyst, the one final question I have for you is:

What's your first move?

About the *Catalyst5 HR©* development programme

Catalyst5 HR is a programme designed to uncover, unlock and unleash restless HR professionals to move beyond transactional HR and position themselves as the catalyst who amplifies HR's impact across business. This multi-day programme is based on the five dimensions of the Catalyst HR model. Focused on *how* you practice HR, with a view to moving from *doing* to *being*, you'll finish the programme a more insightful, unattached, focused and connected HR Catalyst – and doing it your way.

This programme is offered publicly across Australasia with a cohort of like-minded, future-focused HR professionals and can also be run in-house with People & Culture teams.

Who is Catalyst5 HR for?

- HR practitioners wondering "What's next?"

- Those of you tired of traditional training courses

- HR practitioners unsettled by their gut-instinct that "Perhaps we don't practice what we preach?!"

- Anyone who knows, feels or has been told they have untapped potential

- Those who want to do/be/achieve more in the field of HR

Who is Catalyst5 HR <u>not</u> for?

- People looking for a quick fix – this is an intensive programme that requires participants to DO THE WORK

- Anybody with a chip on their shoulder or who blames others for their lack of progress

- Those who can't be bothered looking at themselves and their practice with a view to making required change

You'll get:

- An active network of fellow catalyst HR practitioners to learn with and from, and grow together

- A greater connection with what, how and why you 'do' HR

- Ways to deal with overwhelm by building strategies for letting go of what doesn't matter and gaining traction with the stuff that does (and crucially, how to tell the difference)

- A tailored action plan for your HR practice over the next 45 days post each cluster

- The ability to level-up your ability to influence those who matter (and those who don't so much) in your organisation

Your HR Team will get:

- Reinvigorated movers and shakers!

- HR practitioners revitalised, engaged and clear on what they will work on to take their personal practice to a new level

- A coach and mentor to challenge the practice of others in the team

It's time to step-up and be the catalyst for that change.

Endorsements for the Catalyst5 HR programme

I will perhaps never truly know how important the alarming messages in the programme of "HR is the place ideas go to die" and "Don't be a Troll" were for me in terms of helping me to build and maintain a good relationship with our new CEO.

However, I do often think about... how the influence of the HR catalyst programme ensured that I was mindful of what he was trying to achieve and worked with him to make things happen. The HR Catalyst programme helped me to keep natural risk averse tendencies in check and to be an enabler when it really counts.

– Mark Olsen, HR Manager, Aurora Energy

In developing the HR Catalyst model, Callum McKirdy challenges all HR practitioners to take a step back and really analyse their practice, and in turn themselves, so that we can level up and deliver real value to the people, teams and organisations we work with. Having worked through the Catalyst5 HR Programme in 2018, I can't speak highly enough about the HR Catalyst model and its ability to enhance my practice – particularly when it came to identifying the things that were holding me, and my practice, back.

– Laura Warren, Divisional HR Manager, University of Otago

Get in touch

Want to take your HR practice further, better, faster?

Visit Callummckirdy.com for programme details and further information on how to receive more valuable insights into the changing dynamics of the people profession.

Contact Callum's team via hello@callummckirdy.com for speaking, facilitating and online Catalyst mentoring opportunities.

References

Blyth, C. (2010) The Art of Conversation: A guided tour of a neglected pleasure. Gotham Books

Church, M. (2018) Next: Thoughts about tomorrow you can talk about today. Thought Leaders Publishing

Glaser, J. (2013) Conversational Intelligence: How Great Leaders Build Trust & Get Extraordinary Results. Taylor & Francis Inc

Clear, J (2018) Atomic Habits. An Easy & Proven Way to Build Good Habits & Break Bad Ones. Cornerstone Publishing

Dolan, G (2017) Stories for Work: the essential guide to business storytelling. Wiley

Garner, J. (2017) Who You Know: how a network of 12 people can fast-track your success. Wiley

Goldsmith, M. (2007) What Got You Here Won't Get You There: How Successful People Become Even More Successful. Jossey Bass

Lombard, M. & Eichinger, R. (2000) The Leadership Machine: Architecture to Develop Leaders for Any Future. Lominger Ltd Inc.

Taleb, N. N. (2013) Antifragile: Things that gain from disorder. Penguin

Below

Trimboli, O. (2017) Deep Listening: Impact Beyond Words

Ulrich, D. et al (2017) Victory Through Organization: Why the War for Talent is Failing Your Company and What You Can Do About It. McGraw-Hill Education

Zeldin, T. (2000) Conversation: How talk can change our lives. Hidden Spring

www.ingramcontent.com/pod-product-compliance
Lightning Source LLC
Chambersburg PA
CBHW060933220326
41597CB00020BA/3728